Some of the things being said about Gene and his workshops...

"The doctor told me emphatically that the metastices in my liver would not go away. Three months later my liver is completely clear. I encourage anyone to include Gene's services as part of their holistic approach to healing." *–MK, Financial Analyst*

"Gene is the real thing—he is absolute love, clear insight, and no b.s. As a confirmed skeptic, I recommend him without reservation." *–NT, Teacher*

"My session with Gene was one of the best experiences of my entire life. I feel like I released years worth of pain, anger, fear and grief that I was holding inside. It was such a healing experience, so full of unconditional love." *–BP, former Marketing Director, now, stay-at-home-mom.*

"I came to Gene feeling tired, defeated, and burnt out. I left feeling more alert, more alive, and more happy. Seeing Gene was the best decision of my life. After years of restricted breathing and fatigue, I now feel as energetic as I did in high school. I even breathe through my nose at night—something I haven't done in years! The only question I had after my session with Gene was why didn't I see him sooner? Through his hands-on healing, Gene lifted my spirit and restored my insatiable zest for life." *–FK, Business Development Manager*

"I have been struggling with an irregular heartbeat, which has incapacitated me since my recent heart surgery. During a healing session with Gene, my heart returned to its normal rhythm." *–BH, Pastor, Presbyterian Church USA*

"Gene Krackehl truly IS an amazing healer. Gene's healing sessions have truly been a life altering and transformational experience for me. While years of therapy have helped me understand certain issues and traumas that have occured in my life on an intellectual level, the energy Gene channels created alterations and healing on the cellular level, literally transcending old imprints and traumas that have been lodged in my body. This is what I call healing from "the inside out" and its effect is profoundly helping me move forward in my life in a way that I was not able to before." *–PW, Grammar School Teacher*

"I was very depressed when I went to see Gene. After our session I immediately felt lighter and more joyful. I feel more open and free than I have ever felt before. Gene created a space where I could not only receive unconditional love but give it as well..." *–NK, Teacher*

"I lost my husband 18 months ago. To say my heart was broken was putting it mildly. A part of me never wanted to be happy again. My husband was my soul mate, when he died my soul died. I cried every day and felt empty and angry. Another part of me knew that he was at peace finally and that one day we would meet again. I wanted to celebrate him and what we had together but I couldn't the pain was too great. So, when I heard about Gene I wanted to give him a shot at helping me. Gene not only helped me, I think he saved my sanity. When I left him I smiled like I have not smiled since July 2003 when my husband had the stroke that killed him. I smiled with joy at the happiness I knew with my husband and I was thankful I had him instead of angry that he was taken from me. The next day I woke up tired but still happy. I looked at my husband's picture and cried only now the tears were tears of happiness not sorrow. I feel lighter and at peace. Saying thank you doesn't express my gratitude. But I say it with much gratitude—Thank you Gene!!!!"*—EH*

"In one session with Gene, I cleared old issues and emotions that I had been struggling with for years. The immediate feeling was euphoric; the lasting effect has been phenomenal. Positive changes continue to roll in and my energy increases daily on both a physical and spiritual level as old "blocks" continue to drop away. Gene virtually radiates love, warmth and safety—a rare and powerful combination that allows the deepest healing to occur. I recommend Gene highly and without reservation to those seeking a loving, transformative experience."
–CS, Hypnotherapist

"Thank you, Thank you, Thank you! I came to you with Lyme Disease with the physical and emotional pain connected to it. I had trouble with many daily activities like putting on a seat belt and carrying my delicious 3 year old. The morning after I saw you the pain was about 75% gone and in just 2 short weeks it has just about disappeared. I also feel lighter and freer. Thank you for changing the course of my life." *–JS, Psychotherapist*

"I'm sure that Gene's distance healing helped my mother-in-law. Her recovery, according to her doctors, was miraculous." *–PA, Psychologist*

"Since we met I have had a repeat CT scan and the disease in my lungs is gone just like that! When I saw my pulmonologist and he gave me the great news, I cried, with joy this time and he said, "We really don't see this too often. Usually the disease progresses and this is very unusual." YIPEEEE! Gene is blessed. I can't put any other words to the kind of person he is. I found it so comfortable meeting him, like visiting an old friend." –DN, Entrepreneur

"Gene is a truly gifted healer. Combining both his intuition and his wisdom he creates a very safe space for his clients. He embraces his clients in a very gentle and compassionate way. He has a unique ability to focus on an individual's needs offering them the opportunity to release limited beliefs and old patterns and replace it with pure loving energy. Working with Gene has given me the freedom to move forward in a more grounded and balanced way to create the life I truly desire. In brief, Gene is truly an amazing healer!" "–SA, Life Coach

"There is only one word I would use to describe Gene—a "Miracle." If you are skeptical of energy work you will be convinced of it when you leave Gene, and the miraculous effects long after..." –AS, Reiki Master

"After my husband's death last year, I was in such a state of despair, that I was barely alive. I came to see Gene, because I was at my witts end. It took only one session enabling me to release my unbearable grief. It freed me from anxieties and fears and brought me back to enjoy life again. Now I feel more complete than ever and I have renewed faith in the future..." –RMG, Medical Billing

"Gene's healing gifts and warm, wise, loving insights were like nothing I've ever experienced before—and I have been to so many healers! In one miraculous session with Gene I released years and years of illness-inducing and poverty promoting pain, anger and fear… and replaced them all with warmth & love. I have already manifested a beautiful home—one I've only dreamed of, and I feel physically better than I have in sooooo long. It seems that my wealth is getting healthier ever since that life-altering session with Gene. Where there used to be pain and fear in me, I now feel love, faith and positive expectancy. I whole-heartedly recommend that you give yourself the gift of Gene and share him with everyone you love." – JG, Medical Sales

"I feel a sense of peace in my daily life that I have never felt before."
–TW, Organization President

"I feel the workshop woke something up inside of me. My husband, the non-believer, allowed me to try it on him and he was left puzzled with many emotions. My seven year old son who watched what I did to Daddy wanted me to try it on him and I was really amazed at what he came up with. I am still trying to figure out how he was seeing colors and stuff. He lit up like a light bulb after we were done. If I ever need to think of a moment to feel love, this will be one of them... I am on a cloud!"
–N.T., Social Worker

"I recently attended Gene's workshop on Energy Healing for Beginners. Gene's healing gifts, combined with his expertise in the area and a wonderful sense of humor, provided an extremely rewarding experience. I learned a great deal about the subject of energy healing and techniques used in hands-on healing, as well as insight into my own energies and how those energies affect others. You will surely leave the workshop with a great sense of joy and happiness!"
–SC, Planning & Development

"There are no words to express the joy and gratitude I feel for being able to attend your workshop last Saturday. I left with such a feeling of hope and a smile I couldn't get off my face."–JM

"Since attending Gene's Healing Workshop I've felt far more confident about my own abilities to heal others and have also experienced an increased sense of tranquility and purpose in all of my life's activities. Several family members and co-workers have noticed the difference and have commented on it. No one else's workshops have ever done this for me and I've attended many in the past. Gene is a truly amazing teacher!" –JE, Manager

"After the workshop I felt a sense of euphoria that continues to permeate my life. When outside forces set me somewhat off kilter, I find it remarkably easy to recreate that same sense of well-being by grounding myself and letting that never ending source re-energize me." –CM, Teacher

"I took Gene's workshop over two months ago and that one day experience has completely changed the way I view my life and has made me realize the important role I play in the lives of everyone around me. Simply by learning to run energy I've accomplished more results with my family, friends and co-workers than I had ever thought possible, and there was so much more!"
–FL, Sales Representative

YOU
ARE THE
HEALER

*Discover Your
Miraculous Potential
to Heal Yourself
& Others*

By
GENE KRACKEHL

Inner Place
Publishing
NEW YORK

Inner Place Publishing
P.O. Box 374, Katonah, NY 10536
www.InnerPlacePublishing.com

Printed in the United States of America

Second Printing 2006

ISBN 0-9766987-0-6

Library of Congress Control Number: 2005902166

Editor: Donna Baker Church (awordchick@yahoo.com)

Cover and inside design: Gene Krackehl
Gene@AmazingHealer.com
www.AmazingHealer.com
www.YouaretheHealer.com

A grateful acknowledgement is extended to Maria Bennett
for permission to her image in photos on pages 103, 109 & 119
Photo credit: Jonathan Krackehl

This book is printed on acid-free paper

*This book
is dedicated to
my beloved wife Susan
and my truly amazing
son Jonathan.
Without their unique energy,
and shared lives,
the magic
would not have been
as fulfilling.*

Important Note

This book was written to provide information, encouragement and insight into the area of hands-on energy healing. It is in no way a substitute for medical, nutritional, psychological, or pscyhiatric care but might be used to compliment these and other treatments and medicines where deemed appropriate by those authorities.

Energy healing, like any other career requires dedication, study and practice to become proficient. I often tell people that I can teach almost anyone to ride a bicycle but can't guarantee that they'll make the Olympics. The same is true for healing. Every effort has been made to keep this book as accurate as possible but mistakes do happen from time to time. Therefore this should in no way be the only text you consult but will hopefully be the first of many as you explore the possibilities of becoming a healer. For your convenience a list of additional resources is provided in the back of this book.

Contents

Introduction

If asked what is the purpose of your life, what comes to mind? What have your life experiences been training you to do? With hindsight comes clarity and that vision can often provide life-changing opportunities for the future.

Lifetimes on this planet are relatively short. We choose to come here in order to learn, grow and evolve as spiritual beings. It is my belief that we also agreed, long before coming here, to endure the hardships that each of us receives throughout our lives according to our own unique life plan—a plan that we helped devise. Thus, there are no accidents; there are no victims. Strangely enough, our mistakes and painful situations teach us more than the most successful aspects of our lives ever could. Each time we find ourselves repeating the same painful situation, over and over again, without learning that lesson, we are often met with even greater pain, until our suffering is finally relieved by understanding. We achieve our goal of a higher awareness.

There are also no coincidences. We become aware of them when they happen—and we catch a glimpse of the inner-framework of our destiny unfolding. On a few occasions I've had people swear to me that my brochure leaped off the shelf of a local health food store, into their cart and that is why they called me for a healing. Noticing these "coincidences" can lead us to try something new, to see life in a different way, sometimes changing the course of our existence, leading us to experience and become aware of other serendipitous and exciting aspects of our journey. These experiences bring us closer to realizing what our true life's purpose is all about. Hopefully, this book will prove to be one of those fortuitous occurrences, and might even help you deal with the issues in your life and the lives of others surrounding you—those who so greatly need your help in order to heal.

For most of my life I've searched for something truly meaningful to do. I grew up in a New York city suburb and had a fairly normal childhood. We all have our own inadequacies to overcome, as this is how we learn and grow. I've found that whatever unique life situation you are given teaches you something that you couldn't have learned anywhere else—skills that you will have the opportunity to put to good use at the appropriate time. Each moment of clarity provides that new possibility. Your present vulnerabilities can potentially become your greatest strengths.

I went to art school, got a degree in Advertising Design, and went on to have a family. At one time I was a fairly very well known graphic designer, art director and creative director. My experience was eclectic—from book publishing, to motion picture advertising, to network TV, to package design—then on to my own design firm. At the same time, I taught design and advertising courses at a few New York city colleges and became a sought after guest lecturer at others. Creating unique concepts, designing logos, books, posters, ad campaigns, meticulously tailoring the feeling of the artwork, coordinating the writing, and directing the photography were rewarding, for a while. I was also managing and motivating people while imparting the many skills that I continued to acquire. Almost nothing was more gratifying than watching my creations roll off of huge printing presses in multiples of hundreds of thousands, exactly as I had envisioned them. The resulting scores of international awards and acclamations by my peers, the press and public over many years fed my ego, but I was becoming increasingly aware that they were only superficial indications of success. Concurrently, my ever-increasing spiritual interests led me to explore many different religions, study various philosophies and delve into countless different mental and spiritual disciplines—continually searching outside of myself to find fulfillment. —

In looking back, people have always been my first priority. In my early teens I often had complete strangers come up to me and share the most devastating and intimate aspects of their lives—sensing somehow that I could help. There was an indescribable trust being conveyed there and I always found just the right words to make them feel better. On many mornings, at various jobs, my employees would line up outside of my office in order to come in and unburden their problems. They would feel relieved, then go off and be productive. Outside of work I could sense and alleviate the pain of people by just sending them energy to get rid of their turmoil. This form of distance healing is — something that I will teach you to do later in this book.

Nothing you go through in life is ever without a purpose. I have come to realize that everything I learned in every aspect of my life had been training me to become a healer. One day many years ago I was working out at a local gym. Since I specialize in mandibular aerobics (I stand around and talk a lot), I started up a conversation with the person on the treadmill next to me. When she mentioned that she was a "psychic healer" the light bulb above my head turned on! "Is that *really* an occupation?" I inquired. She confirmed it was and after trading healing stories for a while she invited me to a workshop that she was giving that weekend. I was suspicious, but my curiosity prevailed. I ventured to see what it was all about. After the initial workshop, I started working on people immediately with great success and mutual enthusiasm. Apparent miracles occurred continuously. I had been having miraculous things happen to my clients for many years prior to this point while doing distance healings but always found excuses as to what "other" phenomena had probably caused it. We are taught to invalidate ourselves that way!

I studied with that healer once a month for about a year and over the following years, went on to study with many other wonderful teachers—some of the best in the world. I read every book I could get my hands on, picked up lots of techniques, and continued to learn more and more about energy and how to use it. I've since made the slow segue from my old career to a brand new one. All of my life experiences have taught me everything that I needed to know. My clients and my own intuition have become my best teachers. Throughout the process, I have discovered some simple, yet extremely valuable, secrets concerning energy. I have developed my own techniques to rid a person of fear, anger and fix the broken heart of almost anyone, often in just one session. I will be sharing these gifts with you.

It is my conviction that nearly anyone can become a hands-on energy healer. For years I've been training people to do just that— helping them to help others by working with energy. This book will attempt to show you how. The only requirements necessary are to discover the love inside and have the willingness to share that love with others—which is communicated through your own energy. It's interesting to note that when you focus your intentions on healing others, you might just find many aspects of yourself being healed in the process. Everything in the Universe is connected. Whatever happens in one area will, to some degree, affect every other.

In writing this book, I've tried to stay away from religious and new age terms that sometimes tend to polarize and confuse people. Part of my purpose is to de-mystify the mystical. Furthermore, I am not a scientist nor do I pretend to be one. I've purposely avoided anything that might sound too scientific. There are many good books out there that give substantial scientific credence to energy work. I've listed a few of them in the back of this book. Instead of duplicating their efforts, I've chosen to look at and talk about everything and every aspect of life in terms of one common denominator—energy! I've also included many personal anecdotes and have changed the names, and in some cases, the circumstances, to protect the privacy of my friends and clients.

So what is energy? The simplest answer would probably be to say that energy is life. It's that substance or quality which animates otherwise inanimate objects. It's what allows an apparently dormant seed to sprout and grow into a luscious, delicious vegetable or beautiful fragrant flower. It's that part of our spirits that gives our bodies movement and expression. It's what makes us look radiant and feel happy. It flows through and influences every aspect of our lives, from the way we feel to the way we think.

Over the years, I've found that this energy can be generated and utilized by us for many purposes including curing people of various physical and emotional dis-eases. It's interesting that the word "disease" blatantly states its cause—dis-ease! Stress has so much to do with diminishing health by impeding the flow of this vital energy. By using the methods explained within, I've seen people get rid of physical and emotional pain; reduce and handle stress; change their perspectives about life; relieve depression; achieve weight loss; release fear, anger and grief; feel better about themselves; and lots more. In doing so, they often realize their true purpose in life.

Almost anyone can become a healer and it's my personal opinion that all of the certificates and diplomas in the world won't make you a better healer—only practice and dedication will. As a healer, your unique life experience can become your credentials. You don't have to be able to see auras or other esoteric things in order to do healing work. My goal is to teach you the true nature of energy in a very simple and down-to-earth way and how to listen to your own intuition while getting in touch with and utilizing the love deep inside. Welcome to the journey of a lifetime, your lifetime—as a healer!

Chapter 1

S ometimes the simplest of acts, such as a warm smile, a kind word, a gentle caring touch, or knowing that someone really listened and understood can achieve a healing on some level. Few of us are aware of the miraculous power that we all possess—the power to heal.

Love and Fear

We enter this life, voluntarily stripped of past memories, expecting to learn and grow according to our own unique life plan. Once we arrive here however, we are met with and diminished by the fear that surrounds us.

This fear takes many forms and pervades every part of our existence, forcing us to focus our thoughts on basic survival, even in times of abundance, distracting us from our true life's purpose.

It is often said that there are only two emotions: love and fear. All other feelings and emotions fall under one of those two categories. Hatred, jealousy, anxiety, criticism, insecurity, worry, guilt and anger are all driven by fear. Compassion and yearning for peace, for example, are products of love. Fear cannot exist in the presence of love, just as darkness cannot exist in the presence of light. So when we tap into our limitless reservoir of caring and compassion we are allowing our love to transform fear. Each of us has the ability to touch the lives of others in our own unique and remarkable way, the depth and breadth of which is orchestrated by our intentions, imaginations, creativity, knowledge, wisdom, compassion, intensity of feeling and the skill of knowing when and how to deliver that love. In doing so we may recapture glimpses of our true purpose for being here.

Many Levels

Since we all have physical, mental, emotional and spiritual components, it's important to note that whatever adversely affects us on any one of those levels, if left unresolved, may eventually infect us on all other levels. We all have experienced times when we just couldn't face a situation and instead looked away, saying to ourselves "I just can't deal with that now"—giving our own energy to the situation we're avoiding—only to have it appear more ominous to us at a future time.

A man who was having heart trouble came to see me for a healing recently. As he sat down I could sense his broken heart immediately. After spending a few moments talking with him, he told me his condition began three years previously—soon after his wife died. When asked if he had taken time to grieve, he responded that his solution to the pain was to self medicate with alcohol. This is a perfect example of how "heartbreak" was experienced on an emotional level; the painful grief and emotion wasn't released and as a result, it seeped into the body causing a literal heartbreak—a heart attack.

The body can often serve as a marvelous metaphor, giving us clues as to the origin of our physical problems. I've had clients who were experiencing ear problems and upon closer inspection of their present situation found that there was something in their life which they were refusing to hear. Eye problems might represent their capacity to see aspects in their lives clearly; hip problems could represent a fear of proceeding forward in life. Difficulties with the neck could represent the lack of flexibility and unwillingness to observe what's around you. Solutions to neck problems have sometimes come from simply asking the sufferer, "Who is the pain in your neck?" It's amusing how easily an awareness can sometimes be realized. Physical manifestations give clues to possible causes, but a conclusion can't fully be determined without the input of your client, so utilize them as tools to guide and sharpen your insight.

Why People Get Sick

People get sick for many reasons. For some the cause might be genetic in nature, while for others the ever-growing toxins in the environment may have contributed to it. Even so there could be a hidden spiritual or emotional deficiency, which affected the person's immune system long enough to allow the dis-ease to manifest itself.

From a spiritual perspective it might be part of a divine plan— maybe that person needed to become ill in order for themselves or a family member to learn something. For instance, sometimes people who have been caregivers their entire lives become ill to experience what it's like to receive nurturing and also to allow others the opportunity to give of themselves. I believe that some of us agree to accept tragedy long before we come here in order to gain a deeper understanding of loss and fulfillment. This, however, is a difficult, and maybe even impossible, concept to convey to someone who's just lost someone close to them or to someone who is now faced with a terminal illness.

There are no accidents or coincidences. Everything has a purpose, even though it may not be readily apparent. It is up to each of us to discover the reason for the occurrence and the lesson that we need to learn from every situation. Contrary to all outside appearances we are not helpless victims. Part of our purpose for being here is to learn to take responsibility for our own actions. It is also our responsibility to discover our own life's purpose. Could becoming a healer be yours?

Chapter 2

Why Hands-on?

S ome time ago I was giving demonstrations of my healing work at an assisted living center. One of the people whom I had the good fortune to work on was an elderly retired doctor. He had only been there for two weeks but was already starting to feel the bleak isolation of his surroundings. He was fascinated with the energy I was sending him through my hands and with all the information on energy that I was disseminating. He remarked how important touch is. He pointed to a lady sitting by herself in the corner and remarked; "Two days ago I sat next to her, started a conversation and after a while I asked her if I could hold her hand. She said yes, and within a few minutes she started to cry." When he asked her why she was crying she said, "No one has touched me in over six months."

On a physical level, touch, which can be thought of as a way of conveying love, is something that we all need. Research shows that babies in hospitals and people in nursing homes alike can die from the lack of it. Touch can bring about healing on many levels. It's interesting to note that when we say something is "touching" we're usually referring to a feeling being experienced on an emotional or spiritual level. We're also commenting on how this experience is affecting our own energy.

Unless they've been physically, emotionally, or sexually abused, people usually like to be touched. The most basic instinct a person has when receiving an injury is to put their hand on the place where there's pain. When a child falls and hurts her knee, her mother or father will invariably put a hand there and might even kiss it to make it feel better. This feeling of love is something we all want—to be nurtured and cared for.

The Evolution of a Healer

Although I didn't always think of myself as one, I've been a healer for most of my life, doing distance healings anonymously, sometimes achieving miraculous, sometimes subtle effects and occasionally getting no results at all.

Since I'm an empath, I'm usually able to feel what other people are feeling—especially when it comes to painful emotions, probably because these are the feelings that we tend to broadcast the loudest. I eventually developed the ability to extract those feelings of pain, fear, anger and other negative emotions from people around me and use it to help them get rid of those feelings.

Many have this ability to feel some or all of the physical pain, emotional discomforts and spiritual travails of others at a distance. Most don't even realize it. They assume that the emotions they're feeling are their own. Often, though, the discomforts they are feeling aren't theirs at all!

I've frequently been asked how I developed this unusual ability. It may have been a result of witnessing my parents screaming at each other as a young child lying in my crib. It was frightening and somehow I felt responsible for their strife. I would just feel their pain, frustration, anger, and fear and absorb all those feelings into myself, which would de-fuse the situation. Like magic, they'd stop fighting.

Through this continued practice, the resulting detriments to my own physical health were predictable—I experienced stomach trouble and fatigue much of the time. As I got older, this survival mechanism set the stage for me to unwittingly use this method of control in many future situations. I would often absorb emotions resulting from the conflicts of friends and it kept me from getting beaten up as a kid by a few neighborhood bullies. I'd simply send them kind and gentle energy as I pulled in their anger (aimed at but, as I realized, not having to do with me) and they'd leave me alone. In fact as time went on, the calming effects of my presence were so greatly valued as an adult wherever I worked, that I would frequently be brought in to diffuse tense situations between people who were about to come to blows. People would remark that I had a unique way of smoothing things over. What I was really doing was absorbing and rearranging their energy. It took years of trial and error for me to learn how to get rid of this toxic energy once I pulled it into myself, and to distinguish between the feelings of others and those feelings of my own.

Love Discovered

I eventually discovered that at certain times, I was able to generate good, warm, loving feelings inside of myself, which I would send to others simply by intending to do so. I realized that my connection to others extended far beyond my body's boundaries. As a result, I could sometimes influence, in a positive way, the physical and emotional states of others from a distance. For instance, occasionally at my local health club I'll see a person across the room on a treadmill looking sad. I'll "tune-in" and start to feel her sadness and sometimes get mental images as to the cause. I'll send her warm, loving energy which emanates from my chest and moves across the room, powered by my intentions. In 20 to 30 seconds that person will usually start to smile— not realizing what just happened or where it came from. To this day I continue to practice distance healing.

Although I never thought of this power to heal as a special ability, I was apprehensive to tell anyone else about it. At best, I wouldn't be believed. At worst, I would be viewed as unstable. Fortunately, over the past few years the climates have drastically changed. The "witch hunts" have subsided and integrative medicine is coming into the mainstream.

Our medical community is beginning to recognize other forms of healing as being just as valid as their own methods and when combined, each becomes more effective. Doctors from the best hospitals in many large cities, who just a short few years ago would have cringed at the thought, are now adding holistic departments and incorporating alternative methods of healing into their practices. Methods such as acupuncture, aromatherapy, craniosacral therapy, chiropractic, nutrition, homeopathy, hypnotherapy, reflexology, massage therapy, Traditional Chinese Medicine and many others. As a result, in addition to my own private practice I have also been on staff at a local hospital's health and healing center, utilized as an energy healer.

The truth is that every one of us is a potential healer, capable of performing real miracles on a daily basis. The only thing stopping us is our own notion that we can't. We are all far more powerful as spiritual beings than we ever realized. I'm convinced that nearly anyone can learn how to heal others. The only requirements necessary are to re-discover the unconditional love deep inside—that divine quality which is our true essence—and to have a sincere desire to share that love with others. Once you connect with this true essence of unconditional love, nothing in your life will ever be the same again.

"We live in deeds, not years;
In thoughts not breaths;
In feelings, not in figures on a dial.
We should count time by heart throbs..."
—Aristotle

Chapter 3

Everything is Energy

A ny quantum physicist will tell you that everything is composed of energy. The floor, the air, your chair, your body, your spirit. They're all energy. Words are energy. So is sound. Think of all the wonderful ways that music helps us express and transform ourselves—by helping us to move our energy—thus affecting our spirit and our outlook. Energy can be absorbed through our tactile senses. We can acquire and be affected by its residues from inanimate objects such as chairs, pillows and other places where people leave behind emotional energy. Color is energy. So is taste and smell. Food is energy and the more wholesome or filled with "life force" our food is, the healthier our bodies become—because of the quality of energy absorbed. Thought is energy and the quality of our thoughts can have a similar effect on our bodies and our future. The latest scientific research proves that our thoughts, which can be measured as a surge of electrical voltage, can change the molecular structure of the object on which we're focusing those thoughts—regardless of the distance between them! Think of where your energy is being focused in your life right now. Your thoughts and intentions actually move your energy, and when movement is created, so are electromagnetic fields.

Unconditional Love—a Higher Love

The essence of healing energy is pure, unconditional love, given freely without ever expecting anything in return. It is the unselfish act of being completely present with, and for, someone. It's accepting them for who they are totally without any judgment. It's being willing to share any experience they offer, including pain and negative emotions, with the intention of helping them relieve their suffering on every level by bringing about a deeper understanding of their purpose in life. It's a connection to a higher reality of feeling good inside, the vibrations of which you transmit to the other person, with the sincere desire for their fulfillment on every level. Feeling this love helps you to realize your connection to everything in the universe. The extremely high vibrational quality of this essence also allows those who possess it to sometimes wipe out the lower energies which comprise illness.

The term "love" is often used in many different contexts and therefore is, not surprisingly, misunderstood from culture to culture and person to person. The Chinese define forty-two different kinds of love. Most people who I've talked with feel that they can't love more than one person. I think that's because they are confusing love with sex. In attempting to further define love within the parameters of healing, perhaps it will also help by mentioning what it's not. This form of love isn't possessive, conditional, limiting, sexual, manipulative, or romantic. It *is* pure selfless intention given freely and unconditionally conveyed through your energy while wishing the highest good for the other person. The receipt of this gift can be described as distinctive, special, freeing, superior, unique, extraordinary, exceptional, remarkable, unusual and phenomenal. It is beyond anything our culture presently recognizes. Because it is a higher form of love, it doesn't engage the lower emotions and negative human characteristics such as jealousy, envy, insecurity, personal needs gratification, criticism, controlling, shame and blame. It also contains within its substance infinite patience, kindness, caring and compassion.

This higher spiritual form of love is the only thing that heals. It's our true essence and is the spiritual substance that makes us who we are. It's that piece of the Divine that resides inside each one of us. It's the essence of life. It's what connects us and brings us together on a deep emotional and spiritual level. It's how we recognize each other on a core level—sometimes from lifetime to lifetime. This substance is probably the only gift you can give to someone that will last forever. It is also the only worthwhile quality that we take with us when we leave this planet.

This energy helps people to release their fears and anger; to forgive themselves and others; and helps them to actualize their higher spiritual potential by allowing them to alter their personal perspective. It enables them to see their entire life as a panorama to gain a fuller view. It enhances the perception of their lives as an on-going work in progress. Our lives are a work in progress and when love is brought into the picture, anything can change.

A Secret Revealed

Contrary to popular belief, the more of this love you give to others, the greater becomes your capacity to hold it. Once you learn to overcome your fear of losing it and send it out unconditionally, even to those people whom you may not like very much, you become larger and more secure as a being. There is no limit to how many people you can love—on many levels—or how much love you can hold as a result. The more love you give, the more you will get.

Love Can Work in Almost Any Situation

I once went to an organization with hopes of being picked to design their logo and annual report. As I met with the Executive Director she greeted me with a firm handshake and a scowl, led me into a huge, intimidating boardroom and sat down across from me. She seemed to be in a bad mood from the start and I knew that my presentation was in jeopardy. Knowing that I was the best person for the job and while sending my intentions out to the Universe that whatever decision she made would be in the best interests of all concerned, I decided to flow loving energy across the boardroom table to her as I opened my briefcase. I felt the warm energy filling my heart and extending out to her like a beacon. It took only about ten seconds for her face to go from a reserved frown to a wide-eyed enthusiastic smile as she suddenly leaned forward and listened intently. I got the job and was later told that they'd never worked so effortlessly and productively with anyone in the past.

Your Aura

You have an electromagnetic field surrounding your body. It's your aura. Thousands of years ago cultures referred to this part of a person as life force or spirit. Your aura is what keeps you from bumping into someone in a darkened hallway, and it's also what makes someone across a crowded room turn their head and look at you when you focus your attention on them. It can be seen and felt by people who are sensitive to it. It can also be photographed as well. Called kirlian, this type of photography was developed in the 1930s to photograph auras. Your aura has mapped out your development from fetus stage to the present time, constantly preceding your growth while giving invisible directions to the body. If you were to take a leaf, cut it in half and take a kirlian photograph of it, you would see the aura of the entire leaf. If you took a newt, for example, cut off its tail, and photographed it using this process, you would also see the entire tail's aura still remaining. What's more, over time the aura remains as the tail regenerates itself, demonstrating how the aura assists the body by mapping out and fulfilling its growth potential. It's also interesting to note that when a person has a limb amputated, he can often feel this limb as though it were still there. That's his own aura he's feeling! This electromagnetic field helps you stay healthy and is helping you to re-create yourself each moment, as you progress through time.

Does Healing Work?

The late Elizabeth Targ, MD, a noted psychiatrist with impressive research credentials, undertook a research project which included 20 patients who had AIDS. She randomly assigned them to two groups: the "control" group, which didn't receive prayers and the "prayer" group, which received prayers from experienced healers. None of the patients or healers ever met, and neither the patients nor the doctors knew who the fortunate recipients of the prayers were. Over the six-month trial period forty percent of the "control" group died but surprisingly there wasn't a single fatality in the prayer group. Sometime thereafter she repeated the study with 40 patients, but at this point new drugs were intervening to help keep people with AIDS alive. This time no one in either group died, however those in the control group suffered six times more complications and setbacks than did those in the prayer group.

Energy Healing and Prayer

What energy healing and prayer have in common is the focus of our intentions, which, if channeled correctly, taps into and utilizes the energies from various sources and directs that energy where it's needed.

Does it Come From God or the Devil?

Some people mistakenly think that energy healing has to do with faith healing, religion or even the devil! As far as I'm concerned it has nothing to do with any of them. It works equally as well on skeptics as it does on "believers," proving that you don't need to have a "belief system" for it to work. A woman who called in to a talk show that I was doing recently asked me if I healed in the name of Jesus. I told her that since people from all religions come to me, and even though I embrace all religions, it was not my policy to use religious terminology or the names of religious figures in my sessions, which might, in the slightest way, alienate them. However, I did tell her that the essence of the energy that I'm using is unconditional love, and if you believe that God is love, then you have your answer.

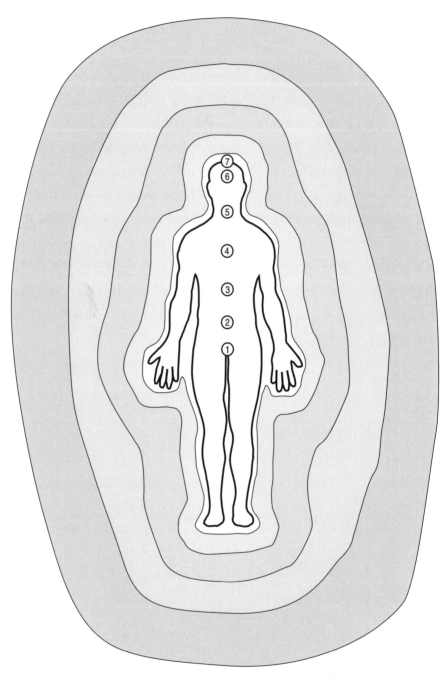

The major chakras and surrounding auric field.

Chapter 4

The Chakras

All living things are constantly absorbing energy from the Universe. Chakras are the areas where this life force enters and exits your body. Translated from Sanskrit, the word chakra means wheel of light. That's how people who can see these energies describe them. Think of chakras as valves. This energy feeds your internal organs along with the rest of your being, which helps to keep you healthy. There are seven major chakras in the body running from the tip of the spine to the top of the head on which this book will primarily focus. (We have roughly 200 minor chakras throughout our body plus others outside of our body). As you become more familiar with the energy system you will also learn about meridians. There are 14 meridians which extend from the soles of your feet to the top of your head, each running through at least one or more major organs. Think of the body as a house. The chakras are the fuse box through which energy from the outside enters the body. A blocked chakra is like a blown fuse—no energy will be going to that part of the body or house. Think of the meridians as the wiring which flows that energy from the fuse box throughout the house. They surface at different points in the body called Acupuncture or Acupressure points and they can be likened to electrical outlets throughout the house.

It's no co-incidence that your chakras are each located exactly where the major endocrine glands reside in the body. The glands are listed with each corresponding chakra in the diagram on the next page.

THE CHAKRAS
& CORRESPONDING ISSUES:

FIRST CHAKRA located at the base of the spine(tailbone)	SECOND CHAKRA located on or slightly below the navel	THIRD CHAKRA located in the solar plexus area	FOURTH CHAKRA located over the heart
Earth	Water	Fire	Air
Organs & glands: Tailbone; legs; feet; rectum	**Organs & glands:** Kidneys; ovaries; uterus; spleen; urinary tract; sex organs; bladder	**Organs & glands:** Stomach; liver, small intestine; gallbladder; pancreas-adrenal glands; spleen	**Organs & glands:** Thymus; lymph glands; heart; lungs; arms; breasts; circulatory system
• **color:** red	• **color:** orange	• **color:** yellow	• **color:** green
Issues: • connection to nature and the earth • basic body needs • physical space boundaries • physical survival & safety (ability to stand on your own two feet) • Tribal: Individual (responsibility) vs. Group (no responsibility)	**Issues:** • sexuality • pleasure gratification • family • competition • control • urge to create • job • financial (low back) • power • fear & guilt • anxiety • betrayal • immune system • chronic fatigue syndrome • Personality Disorders	**Issues:** • self esteem • ego • impulse control • your intellect • criticism • need for approval • center of integrity/ personal honor/ethics • intuition (intuitive survival center) • instinct • anger • energy • courage • initiative • personal power	**Issues:** • your identity • balance • relationships • reality • love–reasons: insecure (fear) vs. unconditional • worry • jealousy • compassion • bravery
Diseases: Sciatica; rectal disorders; varicose veins; leg & feet issues	**Diseases:** Lower back & hip pain; impotency; urinary problems; prostate; fibroids; ovarian/uterine problems; menopause complications	**Diseases:** Ulcers; indigestion; colon, pancreatic & diabetes problems; anorexia; bulimia; hepatitis; liver dysfunction; hepatitis	**Diseases:** Heart attacks; congestive heart failure; MVP; asthma; lung cancer; allergies; pneumonia; breast cancer; shoulder and arm pain

FIFTH CHAKRA located in throat area	SIXTH CHAKRA located at the "third eye" between the eyebrows	SEVENTH CHAKRA located at the top of the head. (Crown Chakra)
Sound	Light	Thought
Organs & glands: Neck; ears; sinus; thyroid; parathyroid; hypothalamus; jaw; mouth; teeth; esophagus; throat	**Organs & glands:** Eyes; ears; nose; pituitary; autonomic nervous system; brain	**Organs & glands:** Hair, head, pineal gland
• **color:** sky blue	• **color:** violet, indigo	• **color:** white or gold
Issues: • willpower • ability to know and speak the truth • directs the electromagnetic field • self control • communication • stubbornness • perceptions & seeing through illusions	**Issues:** • insight • wisdom • knowingness and perceptions • creativity • center of beliefs • psychic awareness • open to what it doesn't know	**Issues:** • gateway to other dimensions • spirituality — need for spiritual contact • belief systems extracted from life • compassion • where divine guidance comes through • peace • harmonious effect on others • divine love • belief system
Diseases: Sore throat; gum & mouth diseases; tooth decay; TMJ; glands; latyngitis; thyroid difficulties; scoliosis	**Diseases:** Stroke; hemorrage; brain tumors; deafness; blindness; seizures; learning disabilities	**Diseases:** Spiritual travail; depression; emotional exhaustion; environmental sensitivities; skin problems; migrane headaches

Sometimes emotional issues tend to block the chakras, cutting off vital energy necessary for supporting its continued growth, thus reducing your energy level and leaving you susceptible to dis-ease. If a chakra is blocked the resident glands in the area might also become affected, throwing the body chemistry out of balance.

Form follows energy. In other words, your body takes its direction from the aura surrounding it. This energy field has always preceded your body's growth from the time you were a fetus in a womb to the present and is continually giving instructions to your cells as to what to do from one moment to the next. This system has never been given the credit it deserves by our culture in molding us as beings—possibly because it's invisible, but then again so is gravity and the air we breathe. Energy healing helps remove these blockages in the person's auric field, chakra and meridian system, thus enabling them to heal more swiftly, in every way.

For many thousands of years cultures have acknowledged and used the subtle energies of the "aura" to heal, from the ancient Egyptians to present day African Shamans. It is referred to by such terms as "prana" (India), "chi" or "qi" (China), "ki" (Japan), "mana" (Indonesia), "num" (Africa), "pneuma" (Greece), "baraka" (Sufi's), "wakan" (Lakota), "orenda" (Iriquois), and "astral light" (Kabala). The mystics in each of these societies identified the chakras and they did so consistently from one culture to another. Hippocrates once noted that "a force flows from many people's hands."

In a relaxed state, when trust and meaningful communication between practitioner and client are established, the movement of one's energy on many levels can be redirected and changed, sometimes enabling miraculous results to occur.

Likes Attract

One helpful analogy would be to think of yourself as a tuning fork for a moment. The feelings and emotions you are resonating at any given time determine the wavelength or key that you are vibrating in. You can be surrounded by thousands of other tuning forks, but only those, which are in the same key as yours will vibrate in response to your own vibrations, and thus be pulled towards you. So for example, let's say that you're resonating in the key of "A" (anger). You will automatically, both magnetically and energetically, attract other angry people to fight with and situations that will aggravate you. By resonating in the key of "F" (fear) you will pull in fearful situations, fearful people, things and people to fear.

Emotions are self-generating and therefore it is possible to control what is being attracted to you by whatever you're focusing your attentions and feelings upon. For example, if you want to feel sad, just think of the losses you've had, play sad music, and before long, tears will appear—and you'll attract more sadness into your life just by feeling this vibration. However, the reverse is also true. Focus on other feelings (which are higher wavelengths or frequencies of energy) such as joy, abundance, gratitude or accomplishment and those people and situations with like wavelengths will be attracted to you.

It is accepted as a proven fact that when higher frequencies like joy, understanding and love come into contact with lower frequencies such as sadness and depression, the lower frequencies are raised somewhat—the degree of which is determined by the power of that higher energy.

Issues

What's fascinating about the chakras is that each chakra has its own issues. More often than not, whenever I energize a client's chakra, by running energy through it, the issue that caused the blockage will surface, sometimes by my client having a memory or re-experiencing a part of past physical or emotional trauma on some level. And when it surfaces, we deal with it together and attempt to resolve it *energetically*. This differs from talk therapy because in doing so we bypass the mind. It can be very time-consuming and frustrating to use the mind to solve a problem which it helped to create. Therefore when using this method, talking is not necessary to resolve the issues that come up. What we are doing is working with, rearranging, releasing and in some cases eliminating harmful energy at its core—at a pre-lingual place, which might manifest itself as an emotion such as fear.

Here's an example of how unresolved issues can block a chakra. Let's pretend that you are being criticized mercilessly by a boss or a spouse and aren't handling the criticism well. One of the issues for the third chakra (located in the solar plexus area) is self-esteem. Let's also imagine that as a result of the criticism, this chakra is now blocked, preventing energy from entering and servicing the organs in that area. That energy blockage could possibly result in stomach problems, ulcers or worse.

By placing my hands on the affected area and channeling energy into the chakra, I can open up the area, allowing energy to flow into and out of it again, thus getting rid of the blockage and enabling my clients to heal themselves. In theory, getting rid of people's "stuff" is nothing more than helping them to decide to let go and assisting them energetically to dispose of it. By "stuff" I mean problems, worries, concerns, fears, pain, aggravations, frustrations, annoyances, anger, losses, threatened losses, etc. That's the simplicity of it!

Sometimes a chakra is too open and needs to be closed a bit in order to function in harmony with the other chakras. An example of this, which I see all too often, is in the third chakra, where our intellect resides. This is the only chakra that needs fresh facts to digest and analyze. It tries to take over for the sixth chakra, which, among other things, houses our psychic awareness or knowingness and is our spirit's intuition center.

For most of us this knowing is an ability which we were all born with. Many of us however, have given up on it due to our "thinking" society which aims to constantly analyze, criticize, second-guess and digest in order to come to a conclusion. When you know something you don't have to think about it, you just know it! That's the difference between thinking and knowing. The area tends to shut down as a result of having to prove in physical terms that which we know on a spiritual level.

Once the sixth is shut down, the third chakra can go into overdrive, sometimes manifesting stomach problems and anxiety. In this case, a part of it needs to be closed rather than opened. Once the chakras are balanced, amazing things can occur in the body. Many of my clients have long since forgotten how good it feels to function properly and when unblocked feel absolutely marvelous.

The Chakras in Detail

If you're having difficulties in any part of your body, please pay attention to the issues having to do with the chakra in the vicinity of that area and see if those issues might have anything to do with the difficulty you or your client may be experiencing.

Please note also that you will find discrepancies and contradictions when going from author to author, master to master, regarding information relating to the chakras, their locations and their corresponding issues. The information provided in this book is my interpretation of conclusions derived from various experts on the subject, along with my own personal experience with clients. In working with people over many years I've found that the chakras and issues don't always correlate consistently from person to person. For example, most people who I've worked on hold fear in their Second Chakra. But you will find that others hold it in their third. Most people retain anger in their third but I've found that others hold it in their second. My suggestion is to use this information in tandem with your own intuition and allow your own perceptions to guide you.

The First Chakra is located at the base of the spine (tailbone). Its issues pertain to physical survival and a connection with nature and the earth. Tribal issues, those having to do with family and groups, also reside here. Breaks in tribal agreements have been associated with causing diseases such as colon and prostate cancer. An example of a tribal agreement might be a marriage or a job contract. Being laid off from a job or going through a divorce are examples of breaks in tribal agreements. It's not really the breaks in the tribal agreements which cause the physical problems, but rather their reactions to them. Things we say to ourselves—that we 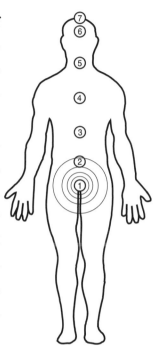 believe—at times of extreme stress seem to be taken more literally and seriously by the body. It almost becomes a self-fulfilling prophecy. It's interesting to see that those who react negatively to tribal agreement breaks are the people who get sick! Conversely, those who experience breaks in these agreements but take an entirely different viewpoint— more positive—get sick far less often.

Our legs and feet are part of the first chakra and whenever we walk on the earth, our insteps are energetically pulling red "earth" energy up into our bodies. This energy is vital to helping us stay healthy. Issues about taking responsibility and individuality also live here. Other potential subjects for the first chakra might be trust, health, growth, choosing a direction, stability, and setting appropriate boundaries. The metaphor of standing on one's own two feet also applies here.

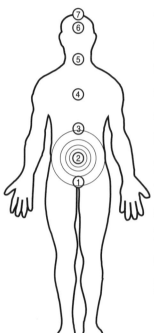

The Second Chakra which is located on or slightly below the navel, contains such issues as sexuality, pleasure gratification, family, competition, control, ability and need to create, work, power, guilt, fear, anxiety and betrayal. If you are experiencing lower back pain you might want to take a look at your financial issues. Movement, emotions, sensations, needs and desires also live here. Personality disorders reside here and your ability to change and overcome inherited patterns of behavior originate from this area.

The Third Chakra is located in the solar plexus area. It's the center of your body's power. Its issues include self-esteem, criticism, and need for approval. Your intellect and ego reside here, so does stress—and of course, resulting stomach trouble. An energy blockage in this area can leave a person susceptible to ulcers, indigestion, colon, spleen, pancreatic and diabetes problems. This is also the center of your own personal honor, ethics and integrity. With a little practice you will be able to feel just how much integrity your client has. Remember that energy doesn't

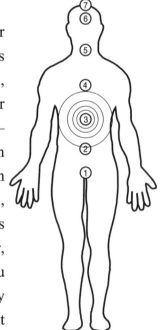

lie! Your body's intuition, instinct (gut feelings), and initiative also reside here. This is where your energy is actualized and personal power pours out. I often find that most people have anger stored in this area and past anger repressed in their liver, which they will have to release—with your help. We'll get into specific techniques of how to enable a person to let go of their anger later.

The Fourth Chakra is located over the heart and has to do with your identity, relationships and your perception of reality. Other issues that live here are worry, jealousy, compassion, bravery, forgiveness, how you embrace life, balance, intimacy, relationships, and, you guessed it, the issue of love and the reasons why we love! We sometimes love out of fear, needing someone to take care of and protect us. Sometimes we use it to fill that terrible feeling of emptiness or loneliness inside. Some of us project our needs onto others and convince ourselves that we are "in love" with that person. Some choose partners who happen to have those same characteristics, which they couldn't work out with their parents as kids, in an attempt to resolve those issues with someone else as an adult. And maybe it is truly unconditional love that we're feeling, given freely without ever expecting anything in return. This is the highest form of love. It is

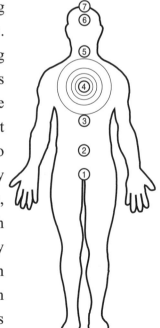

important to note that when we place conditions on our love, it is no longer love, it is more of a manipulation or a contract (giving in order to get).

I frequently speak at many divorce recovery groups in my area and hear so many complaints from people about how they have no love in their lives. One of the things I've learned is that the quality of love we send out to others, equals the quality that is returned.

This was demonstrated to me several years ago. Over the course of my life I've lost most of my family and several friends. After experiencing the death of yet another friend, it occurred to me that I had never told my parents, or any of my friends that had passed for that matter, that I loved them. Having been raised in a strict household where affections were not demonstrative, saying something like this might not have been received too well, and I would have felt embarrassed to say those words to my parents at the time. I knew they loved me and they knew I loved them but my own verbal expression was, at that point, what was missing and what I felt needed to be expressed. Since it was too late to do so I just decided right then and there to call all of the friends that remained in my life and tell them I love them. As the overwhelming majority of my friends are women, you can imagine some of their reactions. I assured them it wasn't romantic in nature but just a heartfelt statement of unconditional love which, much to my amazement, they accepted wholeheartedly.

Over the next two and a half months something very unusual occurred. Three total strangers came up to me on the street and told me that they loved me! It hasn't happened since, probably because I understood the lesson I needed to learn from that experience. The love I was sending out, which was in a verbal form, was now coming back to me in the exact same way. It also occurred to me that not only do we get back the love we send out but all other energies, emotions and actions as well—which reinforces the concept of striving to treat everyone else the way you would like to be treated.

The Fifth Chakra, located in the throat area, is the area that directs your electromagnetic field and contains issues concerning willpower, self-expression, listening, self-control, the ability to know and speak your truth, and your ability to see through illusions. Since time and space are both illusions, energy healing makes it possible to fix situations in the past that caused us pain by sending energy filled with love, forgiveness and understanding to a time and place where understanding was lacking. It will have a profound effect on your present and future.

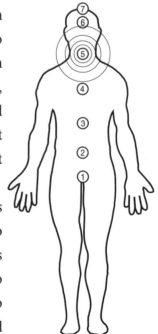

As the chakras open up, your awareness grows as well. You can better discern who feeds your energy and who drains it. And, as your willpower grows it becomes easier to decide whom you will continue to allow into your life—and those who are no longer good for your own well-being.

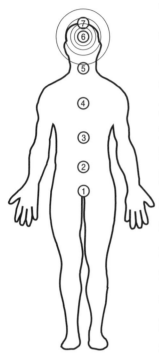

The Sixth Chakra located between the eyebrows, sometimes called the third eye, is the center of your insight, wisdom, beliefs, creativity, imagination, visualization and your psychic awareness. This is the part of you that *knows*! There's a distinct difference between thinking and knowing. When you know something, you don't have to think about it. You just *know* it! Many people are threatened by others' ability to know—their intuitive wisdom. They have repeatedly invalidated and attacked this psychic capability. As a result we have been programmed for many years not to trust this inherent ability.

Imagination is one of the most powerful tools you have as a being because it helps you formulate your future. Without a goal, nothing is achieved. Focusing on your ideal situation while engaging your imagination to produce feelings of having attained your goal, actually brings it into being. This ability can reinforce your intuition by getting you to realize that you will accomplish something.

Long before there was a family doctor or drugs to heal us, our ancestors had been healing themselves naturally. This knowledge is still hard-wired into our DNA and is available to us if we just learn how to access it. Trusting your own intuition is a learning process. Focus on small issues or questions, such as will eating that greasy food upset my stomach? Or will the bus come on time today? Or will my presentation this morning be received well? Listen for a feeling in your body, or an answer that comes in the form of a single thought. After a while you will begin to recognize the difference between your mind's thoughts—your intellect—and your spirit's intuition. Pay attention to the subtle difference between what you think and what you *know.*

Many people whose Sixth Chakras have been opened in a session have experienced a rebirth of their ability to *know.* I received an email from a client about a week after a session. Among other abilities gained she stated, "It seems that right before my phone rings I know it's about to ring."

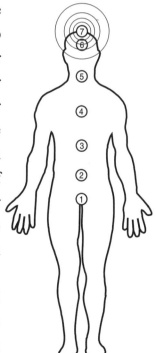

The Seventh Chakra, sometimes called the crown chakra because it's located at the top of the head, is your gateway to other dimensions. This is where your need for spiritual contact resides, as well as your compassion, and where divine guidance comes through. Your spirit also connects with your body through this area. Your belief systems originate here as well as a need for union with your Source. Your intentions also originate from your spirit so they pass through this area.

Spiritual travail, depression, emotional exhaustion, environmental sensitivities as well as skin problems are associated with blockages in this chakra. Migrane headaches are sometimes caused by this chakra closing so tightly that energy can't travel its normal path from your first chakra up through the top of the seventh, thus causing intense pressure. Losing a loved one can be an example of how the seventh chakra closes as the survivor starts to ask why he or she wasn't taken too. Sometimes it closes as the result of blaming one's Source for something or even a person's life's purpose that has seemed to have failed. The harmonious effect of one's spirituality on others can be felt through this area when a person matches his or her frequency of energy to their Source's. The positive and negative effects of your thoughts are also associated with this area.

Chapter 5

Fluidity of Energy

The fluidity of your energy determines how you are feeling at any given time. If you allow "heavy" issues to drag you down, your energy will tend to contract and solidify. The more serious you get about any subject, the more solid your energy becomes and the worse you tend to feel. Solid energy doesn't move very easily through your body—causing feelings such as sadness, depression, and anger.

Life isn't meant to be taken so seriously. If you compare yourself to others who've got it far worse than you, your outlook will start to change. You'll begin to lighten up. As you do, your energy expands and vibrates faster. Your wavelength gets higher and you begin to feel relief. At this point you might be inclined to make jokes about all the things you were taking so seriously before. Your energy expands further and you begin to feel hope, joy and love. The more you lighten up the better you tend to feel. Remember that a "moving" experience is so because of its effect on your energy. It allows your energy to *move!*

Seriousness and playfulness are at opposite ends of the spectrum. I watched Sarah Hughes win the Gold Medal in the Winter Olympics for skating. She was the only finalist to take the attitude of "having fun." Her competitors became too serious, their energies constricted, and their bodies responded at the cost of their own fluidity—and the gold medal.

I had a graphic design business operating out of my home and every so often I'd become alarmed and intimidated by the growing stack of unpaid bills, which seemed to be accumulating faster than I could physically pay them. This situation would frequently lead to a considerable amount of desperation. The more I wanted business to come in, the more I was pushing it away—with my energy. Desperately wanting something is actually sending your energy outward. This is because desperation has fear as its origin. We think that because we want it so badly we are pulling it towards us. Just the opposite effect is occurring when fear is present.

Think of someone you really liked and wanted to go out with when you were a teenager. The more you wanted that person, the more rapidly he or she would move in the opposite direction. By temporarily telling yourself that you don't need that person or job, and lightening up by making jokes about it—thoroughly convincing yourself that you don't want or need it, you can actually attract it—by reversing that flow of energy. Whenever I realized that I was becoming too serious at work, I'd look up at the imaginary sign I placed over my head many years ago which said, "Lighten Up!" I would then turn off my computer, turn on some music, and put my feet up on my desk. I'd start to sing along and do my best to convince myself that "I don't care if I never get another job again." After about 15 or 20 minutes of this, the phone would begin to ring again—with work!

Benefits—Healing the Healer

There's a saying among healers. "If you need a healing, give one to someone else." As you work on other people, you will receive immeasurable benefits. This may be the feeling of satisfaction and pleasure of having given something of lasting value to someone. It may also have to do with the healing energy that travels through you to get to the other person. You actually get to keep and use some of it for yourself!

I have had chronic back problems for a long time, and it sometimes keeps me from standing on my feet for extended periods. As soon as I start running energy through my body into a client, the pain usually subsides and I find it possible to stand for prolonged periods of several hours at a time.

Spirit Guides

If something in this section doesn't fit within your level of reality, then take whatever parts of it that you can comfortably digest and simply leave the rest. If you feel this is too "far out," think of Spirit Guides, instead, as your own intuition.

I view Spirit Guides as Angelic looking beings made of light (which is why they are often perceived as Angels). I get glimpses of them sometimes when working on my clients. My opinion is that they are people just like us who in some cases, incarnated a very long time ago and after many lifetimes had reached a place where they didn't have to come back on the physical plane in order to evolve as spiritual beings.

They are assigned to someone on this or other planets. Each of us has one or more of them. Some are specialists that come for a brief time to help us through a rough period while others remain with us from lifetime to lifetime. Eventually we will all be "in their shoes" as we too will evolve somewhere even higher.

I have, for most of this life, been a "rescuer." Always on the alert to go in and save people from making mistakes (probably mistakes that I've made in the past and learned a great deal from). One day I was parking my car in the local Staples lot as a woman acquaintance was exiting the store and passing my car. She stumbled in front of my car making it necessary for me to jump out and ask "Are you all right?" Now, to back up just a little bit and give you more insight into this situation, I sense people's Spirit Guides at different times. In fact I have an instant agreement which automatically goes out to the guides of every person I come into contact with (I set it up that way). It states, "If you know that I can help your "being" and resolve their "stuff" in any way, please give me any information which will allow me to do so." In this case they indeed responded to my agreement as I perceived them pushing her in front of my vehicle! In a flash they told me that her deceased husband was haunting her, her new fiancé was getting cold feet and that she was worried about her new business. Armed with this newly acquired information I first asked if she was OK. Then I steered the conversation towards her apparent lack of sleep saying "You look tired, is everything all right?" She responded that she was having vivid dreams about her abusive dead husband and she found this very disturbing. I then commented on how troubled she appeared and asked her how the relationship with her fiancé was going. She said "He's pulling away from me and it is making me feel so bad."

Two out of three down! She then volunteered her worries about her business. Within two minutes I got her to agree to a healing session! Other people's Guides will work with you if they trust that you will help that person in their care.

Lesson Learned

I have had two situations recently where I've "rescued" someone without asking first. I was later told, by their guides, that it had taken six months to set up those particular situations and they now had to create them all over again. I had forgotten, for a brief time, that some lessons must be learned from personal experience and suffering a loss may, at times, be a part of that experience. Always check with the other person's guides (or your own intuition) first before intruding into someone else's life. You may have experienced a situation which keeps getting repeated, again and again, each time with more accompanying pain. It may very well be your guides who are setting up these situations for you. In some cases the pain is necessary to get us to have a realization about something—at which point the pain goes away and the situation is never repeated. Of course new situations now present themselves as you progress through your life furthering your destiny, teaching you everything that you had agreed to learn.

Your guides will find unique ways to talk with you or get their point across. Occasionally when I step into the shower in the morning I'll find a particular tune playing in my head. It's interesting that listening to the lyrics gives me insight into whatever situation I'm presently being faced with or will be faced with soon.

"No mirror ever became iron again;
No bread ever became wheat;
No ripened grape ever became sour fruit.
Mature yourself and be secure
from a change for the worse.
Become the light."—Rumi

Chapter 6

Energy Exercises

Moving energy is what energy healing is all about. Learning how to do so can be fun. The following exercises will help you feel and understand the energy in order to focus your intentions on moving it. Remember that energy is often very subtle. The more you relax and trust your own feelings, the easier it will be to feel and move it.

Uniting Earth and Heaven Exercise

Start by standing comfortably with your feet apart about shoulder width and knees bent slightly. Picture roots growing out of your feet as they extend down and out for many miles beneath you, connecting you to the earth. See your fingers energetically lengthening and extending deep into the ground. Lower your body slightly at the knees and scoop up earth energy with your fingers, breathing in and pulling it from deep inside the earth through your body as you straighten up. Pull it all the way up through your body and, while breathing out, push it out of the top of your head as far up as you can imagine. Your hands are now outstretched and open, body standing straight and head looking upwards. From behind, you look like a big "Y".

Now, reach up as far as you can into the stratosphere and pull in divine energy. With your arms moving inward, slowly push the energy with your palms down through the top of your head as you inhale.

As you exhale, push it all the way through your body and deep into the earth, bending your knees, while letting go of your accumulated "stuff" in the process.

Scoop it up again as though you're making your fingers extend for miles, picturing your own roots going even deeper into the earth. Pull in that red earth energy up through your body, being guided by your fingers, pushing it all the way up, out of the top of your head, and up to the ionosphere. Repeat this several times going deeper and higher with each repetition. Each time you should feel the energy flow increasing through your body. Do it in a rhythmic, smooth and easily flowing fashion, just like the energy you are pulling.

Note: I have been doing this exercise instinctively for many years (actually thought I had invented it). A friend recently mentioned to me that it is an ancient Sufi exercise!

Energy Hands

While standing, shake out your hands like you're releasing water droplets from them until they're loose and rubbery. Now, rub your hands together. This stimulates the nerve endings, making them more sensitive and enabling you to feel your own energy. Continue to do this until they get hot from the friction—pretend that you can almost see smoke.

Stretch your arms straight out at your sides, shoulder width and slightly forward, as you bend your palms at the wrist, facing each other.

Slowly begin to move them towards each other in a bouncing manner. Feel the subtle energy coming from your hands as they get closer. Be aware of any resistance you may encounter. At one point you may feel them bouncing off each other—similar to the feeling of two magnets of the same pole coming together. They will repel each other. Get a good feeling for this energy as you play with the bouncing feeling that it's giving you. That's the edge of your aura! If you can't feel it, shake out your hands and try again starting farther apart. Take in a deep breath this time and relax. The more relaxed you are the easier it is to feel these energies. They are very subtle, but eventually you will feel them.

Cut In Half

Once you've found the edge of your aura, try a little experiment. Push through the place where it bounces and cut the distance between your hands in half. See what happens. Most people experience a sensation of their hands being pulled towards each other, as though the magnetic pole has been reversed and is now attracting the opposite charge.

Taffy

Now allow your hands to be pulled almost together but not touching. *Slowly* try pulling them apart. The sensation will feel a little like pulling apart taffy!

Leg Healing

Sit down on a chair, lift each leg individually, feet coming off the ground about 6 – 12 inches or so (whatever is comfortable). Note the weight of each leg as you do this.

Now place your hands cupped around the top of your right thigh, about an inch or two away from it. Slowly run both hands down the length of your leg, all the way to your ankle and foot. Do this three times, imagining white energy flowing from your hands and into your legs with each pass. When you're done lift each leg and see if they feel any different. You've just cleared the aura in your right leg! It should feel a bit lighter than the left. Note the feeling. Do your left leg now and balance them out before ending.

Intuition Training Exercise

Here's a little game that you can play that teaches listening to your intuition: Get a quarter, ask yourself a question having to do with an important decision you will have to make in the near future. For example, "Should I move?" The more crucial the decision, the better. Just for the sake of this exercise I want you to decide that whatever the answer, you will go through with it. Flip the coin. If it's heads, the answer is Yes. If it's tails, the answer is No.

Now feel your reaction to that decision. Let's say it was "heads – Yes" and 15 seconds afterwards, you're feeling bad about it. That's your intuition telling you NOT to move! SO, DON'T MOVE!!!

Partner & Group Exercises:

Energy Snowball

This one is meant to lighten up your energy and that of the other participants. There is no limit to how many people you can do this with.

Start by rubbing your hands together as described in the Energy Hands exercise. Then bring your hands about a foot apart and bounce them together, like you're packing a snowball made of energy. Keep adding to the snowball by pulling energy up through your legs from deep inside the earth and into your hands. Smile as you're doing this and engage your imagination as you toss it to someone else. That person must catch it and add to it from his or her own energy. It should get bigger and heavier as that person throws it to the next person and so on. Use your imagination and have fun with it. After several go-rounds, you can take it and throw it up to the ceiling (or just up into the air if you're outside) and watch as it splatters and covers everyone in the room with happy, joyful energy.

Energy Tango

Face your partner with your bodies a foot or so apart, hands outstretched at about shoulder width, bent at the elbows. Your hands should be a couple of inches apart, directly facing your partner's.

Now, both of you should push energy out of your right hand and pull energy into your left. You're starting a current. Feel it! After a few minutes, stop and try reversing the flow. See which way is easier for you. The dominant hand (right or left) will usually determine the easiest way to flow energy for you, but not always. Note it for future reference.

Now try this. One of you will be the designated sender and one will be the designated receiver. Start the flow going around in one direction as above, but this time have the designated receiver stop the flow at one point by resisting it and see if it can be felt by the other partner. This is *very* subtle energy and you're not a failure if you can't feel it the first few times. Trying too hard can sometimes block the sensation, so just relax. Keep at it and you will feel it. Remember how many tries it took before you were able to ride a bicycle.

Now reverse roles as sender and receiver and see if the other person can feel it too. Learning this sensation will come in handy in the future when you're working on someone who says he/she wants to get better but keeps pushing away your energy. Actions speak louder than words and so does energy!

Mirroring

Two people face each other, standing far enough apart to see each other's entire body. Look into each other's eyes with a soft gaze. Maintain eye contact. The first person starts to move his/her body and the second duplicates that person's mirror image and moves accordingly. After a short while the second person takes his/her turn moving and the first duplicates the moves. They switch back and forth until finally, both move as one, each taking the cue from the other person.

This exercise helps a person learn to become sensitive to others by feeling their energy, thus working in harmony with them. Our energy flows in accord with our bodies and thoughts. After a while you might even feel that you are picking up the thoughts of the other person.

Mime Transformation Energy

This can be done with two or more people standing in a circle. The first person uses energy, like a mime, and makes something out of it, demonstrates what it is, then passes it to the next person. That person takes the "object," uses it in the same manner, then transforms it into something else. He/she then uses it and passes it to the next person, and so on. People have made cars to drive in, juggling balls, musical instruments, trees, food, etc. Everything is energy! Have fun with it and lighten up.

Feeling Another's Chakras

Have your partner lie on their back, perhaps on a couch, massage table or an exercise mat on the floor. Take in a few deep, calming breaths. Shake out your hands until they feel very loose. Stand beside the person, placing your hand about a foot or less away from the body. Slowly move your hand down the center of the person's body from the head to the tip of the spine. Notice if you can sense any differences from one part of the body to the other. These differences may come in the form of temperature changes or other sensations. Most people can feel warm areas; others may feel a movement, like a mini fan blowing. Everyone's nervous system is different and each of us perceives the physical world in different ways. Try the other hand and see if it is more sensitive. The one that is most sensitive is the one that you will use to "scan" with in the future. Pay attention to the "signals" which your body is giving you. Sometimes my palm will start to burn or tingle and at other times I may feel a slight twitch in my hand. Eventually you'll get to the point where you can sense a blocked chakra, or one that is too open—out of balance with the intensity of the others—even without using your hands.

Allow My Energy Body to Teach Yours

It's an accepted fact that a lot of genetic and emotional information is passed down to us while in our mother's womb. Thus, since we have all been formed inside the auric field of our mothers, it stands to reason that a lot of information from our mother's auric field is passed into ours during the fetal stage. The Energy Body is the first level of your auric field, which is closest to your body. It normally extends out about a half inch from the body and is at this level where you feel sensations, pain and pleasure, relating to the physical body

With a partner sitting on the back edge of the width of your table (if you don't have a table just have them stand), stand behind the person's back so that your chakras line up with his/hers. You might have to stand on a stool if that person is taller or crouch down slightly if he/she is smaller. Place your hands around that person, on or a couple of inches away from their affected organs, depending on which organs are affected. Extend your Energy Body into theirs. Use your imagination and watch as your organs, heart, lungs, pancreas, liver, etc. expand energetically to fill the space that those of your clients are now occupying. Ask your guides, and theirs, to allow your body to teach their body how to function properly again. This is assuming that your organs are functioning normally. It should only take about 15 minutes but if done right can make a world of difference.

Group Energy Exercise

Begin by standing in a circle, holding hands—right hand up, left hand down. The first person sends out energy in the form of a short squeeze to the left. The next person passes it on. Follow it as it goes around the room until it comes back to the first person, who repeats it again. This time, however, the next person does something different to pass on the energy (different movement, pat on back, throw it to next person, etc.). You're only limited by your own creativity and imagination.

Circle of Healing Light

Again the group holds hands in a circle, but now all are pulling energy from the earth at the same time while sending it through each other in a counter-clockwise direction, clearing out each other's old "stuff" and welcoming in new energy. Visualize your Source and send your energy to your Source to give thanks. This is a great way to invite an abundant return flow of energy from your Source. Visualize a column of light coming down from your Source in the center of the circle. Psychically place people who you'd like to see healed in the center of that light. You can say their names out loud if you'd like or place them there silently. Add to the intensity of this circle with your love. After a while visualize the column of light widening to encompass everyone in the circle. End with everyone coming closer and having a group hug.

Conga Line

You can do this with groups of up to a dozen or more people.

One person lies on a massage table or sofa. Place your hands on or slightly above the person, wherever you feel they need the energy. Let your intuition guide you. Ask the person to focus on their own awareness of the energy being sent to them. Now, another person stands behind you with their hands on your shoulders, sending energy through you to the person on the table. Not only will you feel the energy but the person on the table should, as well. One at a time, add additional people to the line until you have everyone in the room flowing energy. After a few minutes, the person on the table gets up and goes to the back of the line. The next person (you) gets on the table and the process continues until everyone gets a turn on the table.

Awareness Exercise

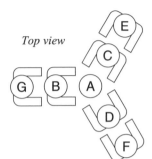

Top view

Here are the positions:

- Person A is seated in a chair, eyes closed.
- Person B is behind him/her with hands 2 to 3 inches from person A's head, flowing loving energy to A.
- Person C is standing in front, slightly to the right while facing A with hands outstretched a few inches from A's head.
- Person D is to the left of C doing the same.
- Person E is standing behind C with hands outstretched a few inches from C's head or shoulders.
- Person F is behind D doing likewise.
- Person G is standing behind B also doing the same thing.

Each person sends loving energy to the person in front of them and is tuning in to the person seated in the chair. See if you can pick up any feelings being experienced by person A. This is an awareness exercise and the person in the chair will definitely feel a great deal of heat!

Take turns in each position and share your experiences when everyone is finished.

Healing Hugs

Hugging is one of the most underrated forms of communication. When you hug someone, you can feel their life force mingle with your own. There are ways in which you can enhance the closeness.

First, always ask permission to hug your partner in the same manner that you would want to get permission to touch a person whom you are working on. You obviously need to use good judgement when working within another person's boundaries. While hugging someone, line up your chakras so they're facing each other. This may be difficult if there are large differences in height so having the taller person crouch slightly to adjust may be necessary. If differences in heights are too pronounced, just intend that the energy from your corresponding chakras is going to your partner's. Slowly and consciously focus on each chakra, from the first on up to the fourth, intending to deliberately open up each of your own as you go. This will in turn open the other person's chakras and the feeling will be instant and mutual. As you open the heart chakra you'll feel the other person relax into the hug. Another second or two and you've made a memorable spiritual connection. You also may have helped to clear out some of the other person's "stuff"!

Seeing the Spirit Exercise

Sit directly across from the person, facing them, knees practically touching. Look into their eyes with a soft gaze. Each person allows him/herself to be seen. Each person is looking and allows him/herself to see the other person. As you relax, allow yourself to see through their body and connect to their true essence—the spirit and love inside of the whole person. Relaxing music playing in the background may be helpful.

We've all been taught by our society that it's impolite to stare at someone. And we've extended that teaching to include avoiding eye contact in some cases entirely. By doing the opposite of what you've been programmed to do, you will find that after a few minutes of doing this exercise, colors and other perceptions will tend to change. You will begin to see through the illusion of the physical world and actually begin to see the other person's spirit. By allowing yourself to be seen completely, you are in essence "baring your soul" to the other person—and the other person is "baring their soul" to you. Likewise, to really see the other person as they are, without "additives," can be quite a unique experience. Lots of things about our true nature as spiritual beings can be realized as we relax and begin to trust. We realize that we are all the same.

Another step can be added after a while if one or both of you are moved to ask permission to touch the other person's hands. This will also help you gain and maintain an unconditional presence by being there totally for the person, accepting them completely and allowing them to see you exactly as you are—a beautiful, radiant spirit, living in a body. You will also be able to view them in the same way and in doing so, connect with them on a deeper level. Sometimes, when you reveal yourself to someone whom you can trust, your vulnerabilities can become your strengths. This is probably because we all have them and therefore can relate to them so deeply. By viewing the rest of the universe in this way we can see how perfect everything is in its imperfections. Beauty is all around us and pervades everything we do and are. By surrendering to it, that reality actually becomes part of us.

This exercise can be a wonderful preparation for meeting with and feeling comfortable in the presence of your client. Establishing that deeper connection is what we'll be addressing in the next chapter.

Chapter 7

The Consultation

Achieving Unconditional Presence

I've found that it's a lot easier to be fully present for a complete stranger than for a member of your own family. Everyone has the need to be heard and to feel that they've been listened to, and in order to do that you have to be there completely for them. Sometimes after a long day of spending many intensive hours patiently listening to my clients, moving and absorbing negative energy while helping them to get rid of their "stuff," I will sit down to relax in front of the TV. There may be an interesting movie or a compelling show that takes me away from "all of that" for a little while. I affectionately call this practice "mindlessness."

My wife will sometimes come into the room, needing to share something about a situation that has been aggravating her or just wanting to talk. After giving everyone else my undivided attention all day long, and quite often into the evening as well, she feels entitled to some attention too, which is perfectly understandable. First she'll start to talk over the TV from the side of the room. Distracted by her, I'll listen for a couple of seconds, briefly acknowledging her and then get back to my movie. Not feeling that she was fully heard, she now angles in closer, trying in vain once again to get my attention. Eventually she is standing in between the TV and myself. In the past my solution was to dismiss her with a another quick acknowledgement, while craning my neck to see the screen around her—which doesn't work, and from personal experience I can tell you that turning up the volume will in *no* way solve the problem! However, making the "supreme sacrifice" of turning off the TV for a few minutes gives me enough time to *fully* be there and address her concerns.

To really listen, letting the person sense that you feel what they're feeling and understand them without judging, rejecting their views or being compelled to offer a solution to their dilemma is what's needed. This is what unconditional presence is all about—it's a quality of your being. I've learned that if I can be fully present for my clients, I should strive to be there for everyone else in my life as well. Each person is a unique gift to you and is in your life for a purpose. They're here to teach you something! When you fail, for instance, by allowing that relationship to dissolve, you will energetically attract someone new who has those same characteristics as your previous partner. People do this all the time when they choose marriage partners who have the same characteristics as that parent with whom they could never resolve their "stuff." Either way you're going to have to find out what's lacking in your own consciousness, make adjustments accordingly and learn from the experience. So accept that person for the beautiful spiritual being that she or he is, be open to learning what they have to teach you and honor them for being in your life. Of course, it's also important to set aside some time for yourself too! Enjoy what each day brings into your life, appreciate all that you have and don't focus on what you don't have. It's the major difference between being content and miserable.

Asking the Right Questions

A consultation with your client is necessary before beginning a healing session. It is so important to establish a trusting relationship before you start to work on that person. By asking penetrating, but not intrusive, questions, you not only show that you're interested but also that you care. Key to the client's ability to open up is establishing confidentiality—that nothing said in a session will ever be repeated by you. Insight into the client's issues, as well as a working knowledge of the chakras will lead you to the area most in need of energy work— even if you're not sensitive enough yet to feel the blockage in their energy systems.

Beginning healers sometimes get hung up on energy. They want to be able to see auras or do fantastic things with energy and in so doing miss the point. I always teach people to observe what's in front of them. Everything is energy. That includes the body. If a person's eyes are obviously red from crying or their body language is screaming something out to you, don't ignore it. Your ability to see auras or spirits or anything else has no bearing on how good a healer you are or will become. *Everyone* is capable of learning to do energy healing!

A few questions you might ask:

- What's happening in your life right now?
- Are there any current physical or emotional challenges which you're facing?
- Have you had any major losses?
- Are there any present situations that haven't resolved?
- How is your family life, marriage, relationship with children and parents?
- Are you happy with the direction your life is taking?
- Is there anything that's keeping you from feeling happy and fulfilled?
- One that I use a lot: If you could have any gift as a result of this healing session, benefiting any aspect of yourself, either physically, mentally, emotionally or spiritually, what would it be? Some will ask if they could have three!

Please realize that these questions are only suggestions, and that your main goal is to reassure your clients that they made the correct decision by coming to see you in the first place. Just relax and be there unconditionally, patiently listening to them as well as to your own intuition. Always make that person feel good about him/herself and their situation. Your total and unconditional acceptance will pave the way for a healthy and rewarding healing relationship.

Once you determine what needs to be fixed, you will need to decide the best healing approach, from a spiritual perspective. Finding out about the client's beliefs is a good place to start. You might ask one or more of the following:

- What are your religious or spiritual beliefs?
- Do you believe in a "higher power"?
- If so, is that power benevolent or vengeful?
- Do you believe in life after death?

The point here is to work respectfully within your client's belief or reality system and to speak his or her language. To do otherwise may alienate your client and prevent them from receiving healing energy. It may also damage your reputation or credibility.

Bypassing the Mind

Your job as an energy healer is not to act as a psychotherapist, even if you are one. You are attempting to solve problems energetically, with little or no dialogue. By energetically bypassing the mind, focusing on the raw emotional energy, we can go straight to the core issue, which is composed of energy. The initial purpose of the interview is just to find a place to start. As you work, the important issues will surface all by themselves. But only those which the person is ready to confront and resolve will become available.

Sometimes you need to "lift" off one layer of "stuff" at a time. As one lifts, the person will feel a great relief, only to find, a few days later, the layer beneath has surfaced to replace the one you've just dissolved. Another session will be needed at some point in the future to deal with that newly exposed layer.

Once the person has begun to open up, you will be given valuable information on which to focus. Usually my clients will give up a physical problem, such as poor digestion, before they feel comfortable about volunteering an emotional loss. The physical problem may, however, lead you to its emotional cause.

Feelings as Metaphors

Let's say that someone comes to you with asthma. Initially you may ask your client what effect this disease is having on their body. Their answer might be that they feel like they're being smothered or overwhelmed. You might ask if there is a situation in their life causing them to feel this way. Usually they will realize that there is. You can make a mental note to check the fourth chakra (heart area) because that's the chakra in the vicinity of the apparent ailment—the lungs. You can almost bet that it will be blocked! Even if you can't feel energy yet you know that this chakra, and its associated emotional issues, will need work.

While working on the person, you're in communication with the whole being (physical, mental, emotional and spiritual), so as long as they are communicating and you're helping them to explore various aspects of themselves, you are working on all of the levels. Sometimes you will find that it's only one level that's affected but most often the emotions will have a lot to do with the problem. While conducting the session, allowing them the opportunity to let go of their emotions will bring relief. Have plenty of tissues on hand.

Starting to Run Energy

In the previous chapter you've done energy exercises to help expand your awareness of energy and how to move it. Furthermore, every time you've expressed a compassionate thought, gotten enthusiastic about someone or something, thrown a baseball, eased someone's grief with a kind word, or patted someone on the back, you were also running (or *moving*) energy.

The quality of the energy that you give to someone, plus the relationship that is built between you and the recipient, has more to do with the outcome of the treatment than any given technique. This is so because the energy that you are giving to the other person consists of unconditional love and the recipient can actually feel this substance as it enters them. Since it's something that we all need, by doing so you are establishing a very deep, trusting relationship, which will enable the recipient to feel comfortable enough with you to share and eventually surrender their "stuff." It's odd that as beings we all need something to hold onto even if it's painful as we'd rather have something than nothing. The acceptance of this warm, loving energy becomes a nice substitute for that pain which they eventually become willing to let go of.

Breathe

The first thing to do is simply breathe! Most of us have forgotten how to breathe correctly. When you breathe, you are accepting life. Practice inhaling slow, full breaths through your nose, filling up your belly, not your chest, with air (which is also energy). Breathe out completely through your nose or mouth. You can't help but feel a little more relaxed with each breath. Visualize yourself breathing in relaxation and breathing out problems, worries, concerns, fears, pains, aggravations, frustrations, annoyances, anger and losses—all the stuff that keeps us from "being here" completely and enjoying life. Breathe in the future and breathe out the past.

Relax

Doing this can really help you to relax. The more relaxed you are, the easier it will be for you to move your energy and the more inclined your client will be to feel relaxed in your presence. Many of my students worry if they're running energy correctly. I tell them that even if they knew nothing about energy work and would just be there, patiently listening and comforting the other person with their calm presence (and their own auric field which is enveloping them), they'd certainly accomplish more for that person than if they had done nothing. You really can't do any harm using loving energy.

Meditation is also another form of relaxation. It calms and trains the mind and body, helping us to release our "stuff." There are many forms of meditation and they can be practiced in an infinite number of ways. You simply need to pick the form that feels best to you. There are sitting meditations such as breath counting, using mantras, focusing on an object, focusing on nothing or on everything! Meditating while listening to music or following a guided visualization are examples of other forms. When practiced long enough, some people even achieve the ability to leave their bodies. This is when you may fully realize that you are a spirit living in a body!

A Simple Meditation

Here is a simple sitting meditation that anyone can do. Find a relaxing place with no distractions. Sit upright in a cross-legged manner (if you are able), otherwise a comfortable upright chair will do. Playing soft, relaxing music may help. Take in a few deep breaths and with each exhalation you are feeling more and more relaxed.

Now begin to let go of all the stress and tension you have acquired throughout the day. If a stressful thought comes in, calmly acknowledge it and watch it float away. Resisting only gives more energy to that which you resist, so gently allow thoughts to flow through you and away from you when they arise. Now start to focus on your breath. Every time you breathe in just know that you're breathing in. When exhaling just know that you are exhaling. Start to pay attention only to your breath. Quieting the mind is the goal. Turn off your thinking, and open yourself up to another realm. One where time and space do not exist, one where your body nourishes and spirit flourishes! Start out by practicing for two minutes and work your way up to thirty.

Walking Meditation

For those of you who can't sit still long enough to get relaxed, maybe walking meditation is more suited to you. In his book, *The Long Road Turns To Joy*, Thich Nhat Hanh describes walking meditation in this way: "We walk slowly, in a relaxed way, keeping a light smile on our lips. When we practice this way, we feel deeply at ease, and our steps are those of the most secure person on Earth. All our sorrows and anxieties drop away, and peace and joy fill our hearts."

Don't try to control your breathing or walking, just walk aimlessly and be in the present moment. When we're completely in the present, our thoughts can't be in the past—connecting to and bringing forward our "stuff," which makes us feel bad without even knowing why. Practicing mindfulness and knowing when you're breathing in or out can help to keep you in present time and more aware.

Take a Grape

Practice mindfulness the next time you eat. Take a piece of food in your hand, a grape perhaps. Feel the love inside of you travel from your heart down through your arms to your hands and into that grape. Your energy is actually transforming the energetic makeup of that grape—you might even be able to sense this. Place it in your mouth, feel its texture on your tongue and after holding it there for a while, very consciously bite down slowly. Feel the juices flowing into your mouth. Food is energy, so be cognizant of the energy from that grape transferring to your body. Each time you chew, know that you are chewing and chew your food more than you ordinarily would. Be sure to taste your food each time you take a bite and enjoy each morsel. See if this practice has any effect on your indigestion.

There are also forms of standing meditation. One is called Qigong—pronounced "chee-gong." This is an ancient Chinese system of stances, breathing techniques and meditations done while standing for extended periods of time. There are literally thousands of styles to choose from and each helps the practitioner connect with and draw from the energies surrounding them, especially those from the earth.

Any practice, if it feels good to you, is benefiting you and is thereby helping to move your energy. Yoga, Tai-Chi, Tantra, running, weightlifting, or simply taking long walks in the woods, admiring and absorbing the beauty all around can also be considered forms of meditation and distinct ways of moving and connecting with energy. You don't have to be a master at any of the practices mentioned above. You only need a sincere desire to connect.

Using Other Sources of Energy

Ever wonder why a home team often has an advantage when playing home games? Their fans' energy outnumbers and overpowers the opposition and the players' absorb it and use it. The more people you have rooting for you, the more energy you have to utilize. It's the same with motivational speakers, politicians and religious figures. They get a lot of their energy from the group surrounding them. The more excited they make the group, the more energy is available to them. Nature has always been a wonderful way to acquire energy. Some people utilize energy from the moon. Because trees are rooted deep in the earth and their leaves reach higher to the sky than we do they also make a perfect source of energy. My personal favorite is absorbing energy from electrical storms. Look around you and see how many potential energy sources you have at your disposal.

Connecting with the Energy

Our intentions are the most important quality that we possess because they direct and focus our thoughts to move our energy. Try lifting your arm out to your side, then overhead. Now, do it again, but this time notice that before it moves, you have the intention to move it. Next, your thoughts tell your muscles to contract. Action then follows thought and your arm moves. You can consciously move your energy across the room, across the street or across the universe and it will do just that if you fully intend it to do so.

Because everything is energy and you are surrounded by it, you are, in a sense, already connected. You are capable of far more, in terms of moving energy, than you've ever dreamed possible.

Break from the Ego

In his book *The Power of Intention*, Dr. Wayne Dyer states in an insightful way that the ego is what prevents us from connecting with our Source and the rest of the Universe. "It's the part of us which believes that its possessions, achievements and reputation define it and that it is separate from everyone, everything and from God." He also says that "Ego is simply an idea of who you are that you are carrying around with you." The biggest problem we have as human beings is that we're spirits living in bodies and that phenomenon gives us the illusion that we're separate from everyone else. We are not! We are a part of everything. Everything is subtly but intimately connected. Achieving independence from the ego is what must happen in order to feel a part of everything around you.

The ego can get in the way of your healing work if you make the mistake of equating your success rate with how good a healer you and others *think* you are. Know that by just being there, ready to do whatever has to be done, you are doing what you were put here to do. As a matter of course, miracles will happen in many forms. Your Source (God, Goddess, The Universe, A Higher Power, or whatever term you happen to use) is working through you to achieve whatever result is required. Just accept whatever that outcome might be, knowing that you're doing your job—and doing it very well!

Suggestion: One rule of thumb I use when teaching energy work is, as a beginner when working on anyone's issues, it's advisable to avoid working on people who have the same issues as those which you've not resolved in your own life. If you do, this will make it difficult for you to distinguish between your own feelings and someone else's, resulting in an inability to let go of it. In addition to bringing up your own deep-seated past upsets, you may also have a problem maintaining your objectivity when working with that client, which may color your judgement and make you less effective as a practitioner.

Lasting Effects

Once your client's "stuff" is eliminated, they will have reached a state of being that they might not have experienced before—one of peace and serenity. For some it can last years without further treatments. Others may need to get another treatment in a week. It is unrealistic to expect any approach to have a lasting effect as long as the client remains connected to people and situations that attack and negatively affect their newly attained level of tranquility and composure. Your client's newfound freedom will sometimes serve to intimidate these people. At that point they may need to see a therapist to help them set up and enforce their boundaries.

When your "stuff" is reduced, your own auric field will begin to grow. As you start to feel part of everything and everyone around you, those same things that connect you can also now adversely affect you. The good news is that once you've gotten rid of your emotional baggage it's easier to get back to a state of feeling good, provided you've eliminated the causes of your strife. Sensitive and caring people tend to absorb negative energy in an attempt to diffuse it. Personally I've found that by letting go of my need to change certain situations and instead accept them for what they are, can bring a great deal of relief. It's like pretending to be invisible and witnessing what's going on without feeling the need to interfere or influence the situation. It takes practice. Be kind to yourself and afford yourself the same patience and understanding that you would give to others. Everything is exactly as it should be.

Chapter 8

The Healing Power of Rituals

R ituals can create a sense of consistency, harmony and security that encourages healing. From the dawn of time many cultures have used rituals to celebrate beginnings like a birth, new job, or a marriage; milestones such as birthdays, anniversaries, or religious and national holidays; and endings such as menopause, retirement or death. Even the simple act of lighting a candle can transform an ordinary area or event into something sacred.

A consistent ritual, during a healing session, can have a beneficial effect on your clients. It enables them to relax and focus their intentions, let go of their "stuff" and make decisions which will help them map out and create their future. Special ceremonies for special purposes, such as letting go of one's attachment to a former lover, clearing negative energy from a room, getting rid of a ghost, etc. will become more valuable as situations present themselves. Feel free to create your own. They can be as creative as your imagination will allow.

Preparing a Suitable, Relaxing Environment

Remember that everything is energy. It is important to surround yourself and your client with an environment conducive to relaxation. This will make it easier for your client to absorb the energy you'll be giving them. First impressions are very important. The first few moments you spend with your client are crucial to the overall experience. The area where you greet your client should be welcoming. Likewise, your healing space should be relaxing and comfortable. The mood of the room is very important and should reflect your own unique personality as well as make your client feel comfortable. Although I am not the least bit religious, I have collected artifacts from many different religions, which are located under my altar and around the room, symbolizing the fact that my healing embraces all religious beliefs and ethnic backgrounds.

I always greet my clients with a big smile, firm handshake (or hug, if I know them), offer to take their coat and ask if they'd like anything to drink. In the winter I sometimes have cinnamon-apple tea brewing, which in addition to its calming taste, gives the air a warm, soothing, home-like aroma.

I lead them to my healing room, pointing out the bathroom on the way in case they feel the need before we start or at any time during the session. Once inside I invite them to get comfortable on the sofa while I inquire about why they're here and what's been happening with their lives recently.

The ceiling of my healing room is decorated with blue gossamer fabric, gathered in irregular intervals, and sprinkled with white stars. There are lots of crystals, not only dangling from the ceiling, but arranged all over the room. They have a way of absorbing negative energy while amplifying my own. In a corner I have a small double tiered table which I call my "altar," with a large Buddha statue in the center, surrounded with quartz crystals. If you decide to use candles, consider using only the unscented variety as I've found many clients to be allergic to certain fragrances. Keeping the area "pet free" is recommended for the same reason. In the center of the room is a very comfortable massage table with pillows and a bolster to be placed under my client's knees when lying down to keep their backs flat. Rock salt lamps also flank my client pouring a warm glow and negative ions into the room which help purify the air physically and energetically. Plants, orchids and other flowers strategically placed among the crystals provide another way to absorb negative energy and help ground and relax my clients. I have a CD player and a collection of New Age music on hand to create any mood I might need at any given time. Climate is important, so be sure to ask your client if the room feels too hot or cold before starting. I always have a blanket handy in case my client gets cold during a session. I also keep a fresh stock of bottled water handy in the room as well. Tissues are also very important to have close by, as tears can start to flow without warning. A release of emotion is a good sign and can bring instant relief.

After consulting with my client, I have him/her sign a consent form releasing me from all liabilities (see page 183). It's unfortunate that we live in such a litigious society to make this step necessary but the tendency of some to blame others, and profit, for their own problems is a reality. Protecting yourself is strongly advised. When working on children, I always *require* the parent to remain in the room throughout the entire healing. This is for liability purposes, as well as the child and parent's comfort. Once the form is signed, I ask my client to remove their glasses, shoes, heavy jewelry (huge pendants, chokers and belt buckles can block the chakras), and turn off their cell phones. They are then asked to lie, face up, on the table.

Always ask permission to touch your clients. I've made it a habit to inquire if they have an aversion to being touched, in the event that they might have been the victims of some form of mental, sexual or physical abuse. Abuse isn't the only reason why some people don't like to be touched, but regardless of their reasons, always respect and honor their request. Upon hearing that it's OK to touch them, I show my clients exactly where I'll be placing my hands during the session—so that there are no surprises later. I avoid touching the first chakra and do that one at a safe distance. Likewise, I am careful when working on a woman's fourth chakra, avoiding any contact with the breasts. If your client happens to object to being touched, you can always work on their auric field instead—a few inches to a foot away from them.

I was working on a friend who is a Reiki-Master a few years ago and the session was progressing very well until I got to her fourth (heart) chakra. At that point she acted scared. When I asked her what was happening, she said that my work just triggered a repressed memory of having been "date raped" two years ago, that her "boundaries" had suddenly changed, and that I was too close! I immediately backed away and finished the session at a safe distance for her to be comfortable and feel good again. The body can hold memories just as the mind does, so when working on anyone, it's important to be aware of that fact. Staying in close communication with your client throughout the session can help you resolve any problems that may be triggered as a result of the energy work. though rare, these instances do occur.

Protection

Now is the time to ask for protection for yourself and your client. I usually say a little, silent prayer asking for guidance, such as: "Please guide and protect me. Allow me to be a powerfully clear channel of the highest energy, for the greatest good of all concerned." Feel free to make up your own.

Begin the Session

I always start the session with a guided visualization, which helps my clients relax and allows them to absorb the energy more easily. I also explain that they get out of the experience whatever they're willing to put into it and if a person isn't willing to confront their "stuff" and work with me, the chances of their having a successful healing will be greatly reduced.

I then ask for assistance by saying, "I am calling in your Angels, Spirit Guides, every being seen or unseen, known or unknown who has any stake in your success on this planet at this time, to come here now and join us in this healing." This usually gets a response from the person and their guides, whose presence can be felt a lot more strongly. As you start to work you might perceive a warmth or heaviness in the air, which can sometimes be compared to the feeling you get passing by a sauna or when standing in the middle of a large kitchen when baking.

Tune-in

Remember to breathe and relax. The more relaxed, calm and still you are, the easier it will be for you to tune-in to the person's body and spirit. Now, tune-in to your own intuition and guidance, as well as to your client's spirit guides. Let them know, through your thoughts, that your client's well being is of the utmost importance to you; that if there is anything they can volunteer on your client's behalf that will help your client to open up and resolve his or her "stuff" more efficiently, you will use it in their best interests to help speed up their progress. Because of this common goal, it can be viewed to be in everyone's best interests.

Running Energy

With your feet apart about shoulder width and knees slightly bent, send your energy deep into the earth. Using your intention, feel your roots extending down and out for hundreds or even thousands of miles. Now pull up the energy from the earth through your legs, and into your body, going all the way through it, out of the top of your head and up to the "heavens." Connect with the loving energy of your Source: God, Goddess, Higher Power, The Universe, Ascended Masters (Jesus, Buddha, etc.), Angels, Saints, or others whom you admire and humbly ask to receive their energy. I've found that by simply sending them your love starts a greater return flow of energy towards you. Gently allow that energy to flow down through the top of your head, into your body, filling your heart. Feel the energy flowing from the center of the earth into your feet, up your legs, meeting at your heart, while flowing down into your arms and hands, into the client. Remember to use your intention to help send it wherever it is needed. Just visualize that energy going to the spot where you intend it to go—and it will!

Stay In Contact

Always stay in communication with your clients, whether verbally or just by touch, noticing the slightest change in their condition. Once you've established a physical link to them by touch, it is especially important not to break that link by going outside of the person's auric field. Keep boxes of tissues at both sides of your table so that you can reach them easily. If you must go across the room for something in an emergency, I advise you to consciously extend your own energy field and leave it right there with your client. Your client will feel your presence even though you're not physically there! Remember that your energy, which includes your body and auric field, does what you tell it to do.

Start at the person's feet and gradually work your way up to the top of their head. Many other healing techniques start at the head and work their way down. Your ultimate goal should be to unlock your client's heart by giving them the opportunity to forgive themselves and others. I've found that there is very little chance of achieving that goal as long as fear, anger and pain remain *before* getting to the heart— which will, if you start at the top of the head. Once you systematically take away the fear in their second chakra, release the anger in their third, then release their heartache, at which point they will have no reason not to forgive themselves and others.

Find that aspect of the person to love unconditionally. Remember, no love, no healing. Be willing to accept any outcome for the session. Remember that the final result is not up to you. You are there to help facilitate what is in your client's best interests.

Experiment

There are many ways to work and techniques with which to experiment. Find those that work best for you. We each have our strong and weak points. Notice while you're working whether your flow of energy is stronger with your eyes open or closed. The majority of healers are most relaxed and flow energy easier when their eyes are closed.

Decide whether you're just going to send warm, loving, energy into a person or just scoop out negative energy into your hand and deposit it on the floor or onto a nearby plant instead, shaking out your hands when finished. You can apply this technique to clients who have pain and other negative emotions. It is actually advantageous to learn to do both at the same time. When starting out, if you have *any* fears about "catching" your client's dis-ease, it's best to just send loving energy into them which will dissolve the fear-based problems.

Note: Never do energy work on someone who's broken a bone before it is set since the energy would make it heal in the wrong position.

Also Note: Do not work directly on the head of someone who is experiencing a migrane headache.

Try "surging" energy into the person for 10 seconds and then relax and allow the energy to flow into them. See how the energy changes as it flows down your arms and into your hands. See the look on your client's face—which will tell you a lot. Noticing the peaceful smile on a client's face can provide you with reassurance as to the effectiveness of your work. Surging is helpful when perceiving a large energy block that needs to be removed. Pay attention. Listen to your intuition and spiritual guidance. Use your intention to guide your energy. You may not feel the need to surge very often. Your breath, which is also life energy, can be used to direct the energy coming through your body into and throughout your client. Just focus and "breathe" your energy wherever you want it to go.

Another way to push or pull energy from the person's auric field is by making circular motions with your hands. Let's say that a person has a stomachache and you want to get rid of the poisons ingested. Place your hand or hands about 3 or 4 inches above the particular area. As you are facing them make counter-clockwise circles to pull energy out of that area. Shake out your hand(s) after pulling out anything undesirable. Use clockwise circles to push loving energy into the area when your client shows signs of relief.

Techniques Don't Necessarily Equal Success

This book isn't intended to be a manual on techniques. The number of techniques employed is limited only by the scope of one's own imagination, necessity and ingenuity. Once you understand the basic mechanics of energy, the rest will come naturally.

Some people have made a handsome profit by setting up schools that teach their particular technique as being "the only one" which will effect a change. Although these other healing techniques often do work, they aren't the only ones who do and spending enormous amounts of money isn't necessary for you to learn to heal others.

Trust your intuition. It will guide you where to place your hands and where to send energy. You could, if you needed to, flow energy to any part of your client's body by just working from one area, such as holding their hands. During surgery, when healers are allowed into an operating room, they may be restricted to just working on the feet of the person but will achieve a great degree of success nonetheless. With some practice, and as you relax and focus on your client, you'll begin to better perceive what's going on inside the person. Listen to your own body too, as you may find *your* emotions or other senses changing. These feelings may belong to your client. You may even taste something that has actually been ingested by your client. I can't tell you how many times I've started a session five minutes after I've had something to drink and suddenly begin to experience a terrific thirst. I usually discover it belongs to the person I'm working on. I offer them some water and they always accept. Once they've had a sip or two 'my' thirst goes away!

You will, from time to time, find yourself scooping into and grabbing at perceived black, sticky masses of energy as you rid your client of their "stuff." You are not hallucinating. Just trust your knowingness. Override the inbred tendency to invalidate yourself that comes from a lifetime of conforming to the thoughts, wishes and actions of various groups that are motivated by fear, and use that fear to motivate. You'll eventually develop the sensitivity to feel these masses snap like silly putty when you've pulled them far enough away from your client. I find this particular technique works especially well on people with cancer. Be careful where you deposit these "masses" as you wouldn't want them to be acquired, however unlikely, by someone else. Plants, interestingly enough, seem to thrive on this kind of energy, so be sure to keep some plants in your healing room. After retrieving these masses, shake out your hands onto a nearby plant. Think of it as a sort of fertilizer!

Balance the chakras after you've cleared them simply by placing your hands on two of them simultaneously, ensuring they have the same amount of "heat" flowing out of each and intending the frequencies of each be attuned. Work your way up, starting with the first chakra, doing each pair consecutively. Your intention will allow you to balance them in this manner. I frequently tie the person's sixth (insight, wisdom) to each one that I find to be operating on its own. The second, third and fourth chakras are notorious for this. For instance, the second chakra can hold a great deal of anxiety and fear. Once you've gotten rid of those emotions, it's a good idea to get the sixth chakra back in touch with it to prevent it from acquiring new "irrational" fears.

The third chakra, notorious for analyzing everything and taking over for the sixth, is best served by balancing it with, and intending that it be governed by the sixth chakra again.

You also may find problems between the fourth (heart) and sixth (head) chakras. The fifth chakra (throat) is the area where they do battle! Here again, balance the sixth with the fourth and your client's future will progress more smoothly.

Often you'll find issues of unmet needs and runaway emotions in the second. By tying this to the fourth you can get them communicating again. Chakras often become independent contractors in a sense, working in competition with and without regard for their neighbors. By thinking of each as the pistons of a finely tuned sports car you can do a tune-up to get them all working together as one complete unit— exponentially increasing their output.

Finishing Up

When you're done running energy and balancing chakras, you can manually "rake" off any energies which are no longer needed. Extend your "energy" fingers very long and run them through the person's body and auric field. Remember the last time you got scared and what that did to shrink your auric field close to the body? Well, you can manually "puff it up" with your palms facing up, fingers gently pushing the field out from your client's body at the same time that your palms are running energy. This will make the auric field noticeably larger and your client will most likely feel the difference. Smoothing out their aura is also recommended. The auric field, which extends far beyond the body, also needs to be worked on. You can save it until last. By just moving your energized hands through the person's field, you will help rid them of their remaining "stuff" and smooth out their energy field. After raking and puffing, this can be thought of as putting the icing on the cake. See how graceful you can become as each movement runs into the next.

I regularly smudge—burn some white sage—the healing room to get rid of any remaining negative energy before the next client arrives. Just be sure to air out the area before the next arrival in case of allergies. I also do the "Uniting Earth & Heaven" exercise to get rid of any negative energy left over inside of me from the previous session. This exercise is explained in Chapter 6 and other clearing techniques are listed in Chapter 13.

Without exception, know that every life you choose to touch will improve just by your intention to make it better. Knowing how and when to do so are just lessons acquired through experience. Don't be afraid to make mistakes. We all make them. Love is forgiving.

Sound is energy and we respond on every level to music when it is appropriate to the given situation. Healing sessions most definitely require something soothing to help one relax. I often spend time at my local music stores sampling all types of New Age music imagining just how each piece will fit into a given session. I have music to go with first sessions, second sessions and all types of specific emotional situations. I occasionally use soundtracks from major motion pictures as well. Use your intuition when making a selection.

Some of the music I recommend at the end of the book is purposely engineered to last 50 minutes to an hour, allowing the music to cue you in case you don't have a clock in your room.

"Doubts...often beget the facts they fear."
—Thomas Jefferson

Chapter 9

Tracing the Origins of Our Feelings

Everyone experiences negative emotions such as sadness, anger and depression. Tracing the origins of those feelings is an important part of the healing process.

The truth is that we all hold onto our own "stuff" even though we tend to blame others for causing those feelings. We also take on others' "stuff" by consciously or subconsciously wanting to reduce other's pain in an attempt to rescue them from those feelings. Sometimes we may unwittingly absorb those types of emotions because we are sensitive to the negative energy of other people. This can happen because our subtle energy fields are interconnected. Regardless of how they are acquired, we tend to forget, or acknowledge, where they originated and come to believe that they are our own feelings. Surprisingly, we expend a great deal of our energy holding onto that stuff. We are completely responsible for everything we hold onto— a responsibility we have to acknowledge if we stand any chance of getting rid of it in the future. With practice, we are quite capable of letting it go.

They're Just Illusions

The secret is to realize that these feelings are just illusions. They're *only feelings*. They are invisible recordings of bad experiences from our past that hover in our auric fields waiting to be triggered by a thought, which in some vague way is associated with the experience. I perceive them as tiny, microscopic particles that have recorded every part of the bad experience. Everything that has been heard, seen, felt, tasted, or smelled is contained within that recording. Ever wonder why you're feeling great and suddenly, without warning, you start to feel miserable? Chances are one or more of these particles, magnetically attracted to our bodies, got triggered. These bad feelings can take the form of sadness, depression, fear, anger, etc. Of course, if they are allowed to remain there for extended periods of time, they will almost certainly create dis-ease by wearing down our immune systems.

It is my opinion that these are stimulus-response devices, installed in our species and passed down to us genetically as a survival mechanism. We also take these memories with us, as spirits, from one lifetime to another. For instance, let's go back to prehistoric times, when while sitting around a campfire, you might have decided to stick your finger into a fire to see what would happen, and as a result got burned. As humans, we had not yet developed the capacity to think very clearly. From that point on, your finger would throb and burn slightly whenever you saw fire, or anything else that reminded you of it, instilling a feeling of fear. You would go to great lengths to stay away from fire and every time you thought of it with fear, your thoughts were giving more power to that fear, turning it into an irrational feeling. Many of these bad experiences got encrypted into our DNA because in the past they served us well. Now, however, we can think and reason for ourselves. We no longer need emotional fears to control us in this manner.

Fear is a principal method of control. It has been a controlling factor since the dawn of time. Governments have maliciously used it to achieve their ends. For example, Hermann Goering, Hitler's designated successor was quoted in *Nuremberg Diary* as having said, "Voice or no voice, the people can always be brought to the bidding of the leaders. All you have to do is tell them they are being attacked and denounce the pacifists for lack of patriotism and exposing the country to danger. It works the same in any country." Sound familiar?

Corporations use fear of losing their jobs to manage employees. Our media supports that state of fear by bombarding us with the latest news on every tragedy occurring anywhere, on a minute to minute basis.

Drug companies and the medical establishment use it by suggesting symptoms, which may be indications of serious health problems. The suggestion is implanted by an authority figure, then our imaginations and belief systems go into high gear, like a self-fulfilling prophecy.

The reality is that whatever we focus our thoughts on, we magnetically and energetically attract that energy into our lives.

Doing the "Getting Rid of Fear" energy process, on the next page, on someone in a healing session can be an eye opening, rewarding, liberating and life changing experience. Here's something else that you can do. Words and thoughts are energy. Most news we hear is negative. If you are overwrought by anxiety, try turning off your TV and not reading your newspaper for a week. If there's something really important to be known, you'll find out about it anyway.

Getting Rid of Fear

Remember when you were a kid and how frightened you were at seeing your first scary movie? At some point you realized that it was only a movie and couldn't actually hurt you, even though it made you *feel* scared. Frightening feelings and memories from the *past* are similar. They only *threaten* to harm you. Like a school-yard bully who doesn't know how to fight, their power is in getting you to comply through threats. Your fear makes them seem more powerful to you and thus fuels their apparent power. You are actually giving your energy, through fear, to them to use against you. But if you knew their secret and were willing to feel the effects of your own feelings, you'd realize that the only power they have over you is the energy that you give them by feeling afraid.

When these feelings of fear kick in, tell yourself, "it's just a feeling," the same way you told yourself as a child "it's just a movie." Eventually, as you fully realize that it is only an illusion, the power of these recordings is depleted. Remind yourself that these feelings are an illusion that you agreed to believe in order to insure your survival.

With your client lying on your table on his/her back, standing on his/her left side. Position your left hand very lightly touching the top of their second chakra (navel area) and your right hand positioned under your client's back, directly under their second chakra.

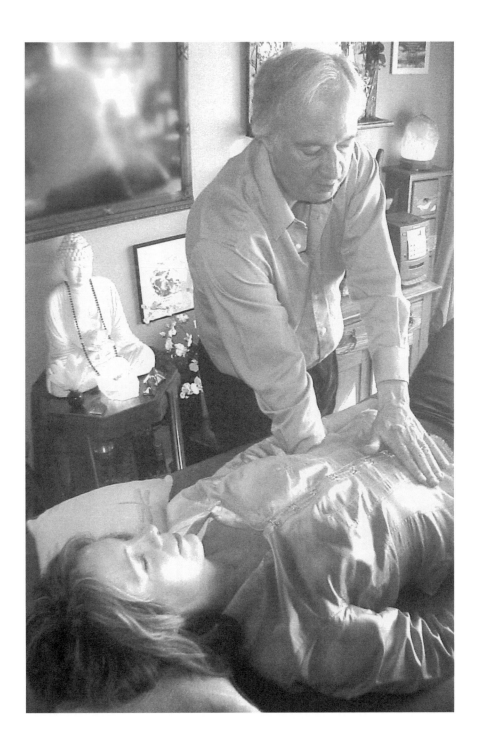

Applying This Principle to a Healing Session

1. Position your client lying on your table, on his/her back and stand (or sit) on his/her left side.

Note: On all of the examples explained in this book, where you position your body and which hands you use are personal preferences based on what feels more comfortable to you and to your client.

Position your left hand very lightly touching the top of their second chakra (navel area) and your right hand positioned under your client's back, directly under their second chakra.

2. Explain the concept of fear to your client as explained previously, then clearly and directly ask the person to close their eyes and go as far into their own core as they can, to a place where there is only emotion. Explain that it's a pre-lingual space deep inside of them where the "heavy" emotions are stored. Tell them that they don't have to understand where these feelings came from (although as you work, memories sometimes surface) and that all they have to do is to just *feel* those feelings—which are composed of energy.

3. Then, with all of your own intention that you can gather, tell your client to "feel the fear." As he/she does this, they will automatically pull those particles (or recordings) filled with fear towards the body and in most cases, will actually feel the fear. Again, realize that this is only a feeling and can't actually hurt your client. Get them to realize this as well. In working with people for many years I've come to understand the true nature of these particles. In a way they seem to behave like static electricity. As you know, with static electricity, if you were to touch something statically charged, it will give you a shock. This shock makes you somewhat afraid to touch that area again. But when you do muster up the courage to touch that spot again, you realize that there is no shock left to be felt. It was discharged with your last touch! These particles that surround us seem to have the same properties. I've noticed that these particles, when engaged, increase their power by getting you to comply before they get too close to your body. Your compliance is what gives them their strength. Since we've spent most of our lifetimes avoiding these feelings, each time we do, we give them more power—and never fully discharge them. If they were to be pulled completely into the body they would be discharged, disarming and evaporating them forever!

4. Ask your client to visualize these particles being pulled towards their body (by the fear they are now feeling) and to be willing to fully experience any uncomfortable feelings. Pay close attention to your client's facial expressions. They will tell you if they are feeling the fear or just avoiding it.

5. As your client fully feels them, these particles and the feelings associated with them are completely discharged. As the person renders those particles helpless, pull or scoop the remnants out with your left hand, while filling the space now vacated by that fear, with lots of warm, loving energy coming from your right hand. Be sure to deposit whatever negative energy you've pulled out with your left hand away from your client, into a nearby plant.

6. Get your client to visualize, and feel, more and more particles coming in (they sometimes shake as they're lying on the table). As more particles are felt—and dissolved—more loving energy is absorbed and their confidence grows. You might even ask them to visualize themselves functioning as a huge bug-zapper.

7. After a while these particles, in a strange way, seem to realize that they will be vaporized and start to move in the other direction. Encourage your client to go after them, either by feeling more fear or by jumping into them, seeking them out, feeling and destroying them once and for all. It's interesting to note that the fear, which in the past was used to control the person, is now being used by the person to eliminate the source of the fear.

8. Useful anger can surface as your client is now realizing that these "buggers," as one of my clients recently called them, have been controlling them for their entire lives. Encourage them to use that anger to feel more fear and vanquish those particles forever. Ask your client to scan through his/her body, especially through any bone, muscle, joint or organ that has been giving them pain recently. Chances are some of these particles are hiding out in those areas. Tell them to locate the particle, discharge it and destroy it forever. In closely observing people, and myself, over many years, I've concluded that most people are basically needy. They need to *have* something, and would rather have fear than the prospect of having nothing at all. That's why you give them loving energy to replace that which they have lost.

9. After about five or ten minutes of this, check with your client to see if he/she can feel any more fear. If they can no longer feel the fear—it's probably gone. In many cases, all the fear has now disappeared—forever!

I was recently the subject of a documentary filmed in my healing room. The client was a psychiatrist who had liver cancer. He also, understandably, had a tremendous fear of dying which during a three-hour session I managed to completely eradicate. When we concluded I asked if there was anything he wanted to share. He looked up with surprise and said "I'm no longer afraid to die!" This is an example of a marvelous healing because his energy, previously going to the fear, was now being utilized by his body to heal his physical condition.

Getting Rid of Anger

In many of my clients I've noticed that repressed anger is often created from an inability to speak their truth—to get certain things "off their chest." I give them the opportunity to do just that. I help them to "psychically" hook up with the person whom they never had the opportunity to confront. It doesn't matter if that person is alive or deceased because everything *is* energy and their spirits are already connected. The person is *actually* contacting the other person's higher self and in doing so is getting it off their chest.

1. While your client is lying face up on the table, and you're standing to their left, start running energy through their third chakra (solar plexus area) with your left hand. First ask if there is any person who stands out in their mind as the one who they always wanted to "tell off" but due to circumstances which prevented them from speaking their mind, never did. Abusive relationships can be prime examples of these kinds of situations.

2. Then place your right thumb on their forehead, slightly above their sixth chakra with the third and fourth fingers of your right hand extending towards the top of their head, touching it while straddling both sides of their seventh chakra, located at the top of the head. Think of yourself as an antenna. (Position not shown in photo). If this feels too invasive to your client, just place your hand above their head.

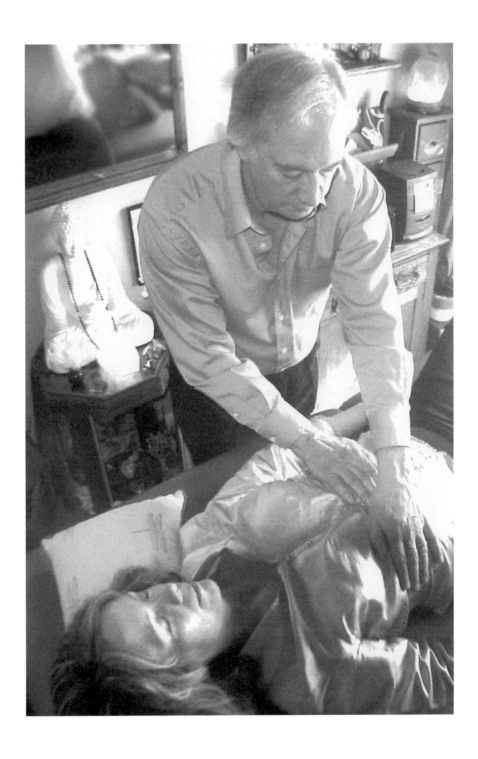

3. Ask your client to concentrate on the other person, using their intuition to locate where that person's body is (if that person is still alive), using the body as a relay point to reach the higher self. Now have them start sending thoughts to that person's body on up through their spinal cord, through their head and up into the spirit and further on up to their "higher self." (If the subject they are hung up on is deceased ask them to focus directly on that person's "higher self"). At that point mention that the "higher self" is that part of the person's spirit which knows everything about itself, including its life's purpose—but doesn't necessarily let the rest of the being in on it. In a sense you're having them "go over the person's head," something they could never do before. If you've ever worked in a corporation you know that power flows from the top down.

4. Ask your client to tell that person everything they always wanted to but couldn't at the time, for example, how much they were hurt, how selfish and cruel that person might have been, etc.

5. When your client is done venting, (either aloud or by sending their thoughts to the other person), ask them to request a response and get an answer—and tell you the response. If your client is satisfied with the answer, have them thank the recipient. If not satisfied, I ask them to use that anger and demand a response. When finally satisfied, ask them to pull back their energy, knowing that they were heard and acknowledged. Quite often they will receive thoughts from that person apologizing for what they did and how they acted, sometimes giving an excuse for their behavior. Sometimes they don't get the response that they were expecting, or no response at all, but they can rest assured that they were heard. I've seen many miraculous shifts in demeanor occur in the objects of these "ventings," as well as the release of long repressed anger in my clients.

6. If there appears to be more anger, ask if there's anyone else to whom they haven't expressed their repressed anger. If so, have them repeat the above steps for this new person. If not, ask your client to take in a huge breath (when you breathe you accept life), attach that breath to any angry energies that remain and very forcefully expel them out of the mouth. Do this several times until the anger is gone.

Spirits in Bodies

As I mentioned earlier, we are all spirits living in bodies. Our bodies are genetically influenced on a cellular level. They know that they're going to die some day and, understandably, fear death. They are an entity separate from us, the spirit. Every time we make a major change in our lives, such as switch jobs, move, or end relationships, the red flags go up and our body is put on alert. The body will sometimes try to ward off its feared demise by creating aches and pains in an attempt to slow down the spirit from "doing it in" prematurely.

We as spirits, on the other hand, are immortal. We've been around for many lifetimes and understand on a deep level that we're never going to die. Our spiritual nature is to go places, do things, laugh, have adventures, take chances, experience connectedness, achieve and excel according to our individual life plan, and have fun! When you put these two entities together, the spirit and the body, you've got a war! Each is fighting for control. However, once you, as a being, fully realize that you *are* a spirit and that your body is more or less an extension of you, your body will comply more fully with your wishes. I think of my body as my apartment, inhabiting it and enabling me, the spirit, to have human experiences in this physical world. One day it will die but I, the spirit, will live on. My own memories of past lives seem to reinforce this reality for me.

Your Relationship with Your Body

I consider my relationship with my body as an employer/employee relationship. My body works for me. Having managed other people in several large companies for a substantial part of my life, I realize that there are many management styles that can be applied. Management through fear is very prevalent in this society right now and has been for quite a few years. In many companies, employees are overworked and underpaid. Appreciation by their employers, which has been shown to be the number one motivating factor for productivity, is often absent. What happens? Their morale and productivity drop, they look elsewhere for work, get sick more often and sometimes die. You don't want your body doing that!

Many years ago I was in charge of a group of creative people in a large corporation. I read and practiced *The One Minute Manager* written by Kenneth Blanchard, Ph.D. and Spencer Johnson, MD. One part consisted of going around telling your employees everything they did right and going out of your way not to criticize them. I used this exercise, in addition to encouraging my people to bring plants, music, and pieces of "home" into their offices. The result? They were three times more productive than anyone else in the company! I was, of course, criticized mercilessly by my supervisors because my employees were too happy. They concluded that my employees didn't have enough work to do. I realized that misery loves company and that they were so miserable with their own lives, the only thing that could make them feel good was reducing someone else to their level of suffering.

I also started applying *The One Minute Manager* to my body. Each day, I thank it for getting me through another day, take it to the gym regularly, listen to it and acknowledge it when there's an ache or a pain. I take it for a massage whenever I can afford it, give it vitamins and feed it good food—which is good energy! Of course I occasionally give it ice cream and chocolate chip cookies—which is a quality of life issue. My body has yet to object! Since applying these techniques, I don't get sick as often, have more energy and in general, feel younger than I did ten years ago. For me, this partnership between the spirit and body has paid off.

Chapter 10

Spiritual Connections

W e are all spirits living in bodies. Our physical, mental, emotional and spiritual components are all connected. When our bodies break down, treating the physical layer alone often doesn't provide lasting relief because whatever negatively affects us on any one level eventually has the potential to infect us on all other levels. In the long term, treating every aspect of a person is what's required.

On a spiritual level we're all connected. Contrary to how it appears, it's impossible to lose the spiritual connection to someone you love— even if they die. Their physical body may be gone, but their spirit still exists. When we lose someone close to us, we experience a great deal of grief and painful emotions. In our grief we hold onto anything that reminds us of that person. We associate the pain that we're now feeling with the person who left. In an irrational way, we hold onto that pain out of fear that if we let it go, we might also let go of the memories associated with that person. Sometimes we would rather have pain than nothing at all. In actuality grief and other painful emotions are sitting in our heart and on those communication lines consisting of our energy, *blocking* the connection to our loved ones.

Once this blockage is eliminated, it's possible to re-establish a much stronger spiritual connection to the deceased loved one. As a result, we may be better able to connect with that person when they think of us, and vice versa. We may be able to feel their presence when they come to visit, and they *do* come to visit—more often than we realize. Remember that even though they've lost their body, they—the spirit— still exist. Eventually we will all be reunited with our loved ones. Getting through that period of grief, while trying not to let it distract us from fulfilling our life purpose here on this planet, can be very challenging. Energy healing can greatly help facilitate that goal.

Connections Are Never Lost

Although I have never considered myself to be a psychic medium, every once in a while something unexpected happens in a session that blows the socks off the person I'm working on and me, as well. A few years ago I worked on a woman who had lost her 26 year-old son three years before. She had been experiencing terrible grief every day since his death. She was awfully bereaved on the day that she came to see me.

During the session we repaired her heart as explained later in this chapter, addressed and resolved other issues. Then something extraordinary happened. Her son came into the room—standing right at her side. Although I didn't see him I could feel his presence, as did she. He started to talk with her, through me, telling her that he has constantly been around her and cited specific examples of when she had felt his presence. She confirmed what was being said. He also mentioned that he left signs that he had been there—glasses re-arranged, possessions of his left on her bed, etc. He also assured her that he would always be with her. She left feeling very relieved and has been fine ever since.

On another occasion I was working on a therapist who had been sexually abused by her father when she was a child. He had died two years before she came to see me so she felt that any hope of resolving her abuse with any degree of finality had been lost. Having had a string of failed relationships throughout her life as a result, she came to me to fix her broken heart.

First we addressed and released the terrible fear in her second chakra, proceeded to handle the considerable anger in her third and before beginning to release the horrible pain in her fourth her father showed up, standing a short distance from her. Although I normally don't see these kinds of things, I could see a vague outline of his energy body. I asked her to tell him exactly how she felt from all those years of being molested—how it shaped and crippled her social life; and devastated her self esteem with tremendous shame and guilt. Not being one to mince words, she let him have it, getting everything off her chest as he stood there, somewhat dumbfounded. After a few minutes of her venting, he came closer, tears streaming down his ethereal eyes. He begged her forgiveness and promised to make it up to her in the next life. They both cried for a while and then she forgave him completely.

She realized that had it not been for her abusive life with him she would never have become a therapist. All the people whose lives she helped would have never been touched. He faded away and we proceeded to fix her broken heart. She also forgave everyone else in her life—including her mother who looked the other way throughout her childhood. The woman later told me that it was the most powerful experience she had ever had—including thirty years of undergoing her own psychotherapy. Soon after, not surprisingly, she met and married a wonderful man and has been doing well ever since.

As I mentioned before, these things do happen from time to time, and you don't have to be a "psychic" in order for them to happen to you. Just be there fully, remaining open to any possibility, while surrounding the person with love. Be willing to accept whatever experience that needs to happen in order to resolve their "stuff." Your "psychic" abilities will continue to increase as your intention to help grows.

Eliminating the Emotional Pain—Fixing a Broken Heart

Position the person lying on your table, on their back so that you are standing on their left side. Place your left hand over the front of the person's heart chakra (in the center of the chest) and your right hand under their back on the other side of their heart chakra (slipped between the upper part of their shoulder and neck). As always, ask permission to place your hands in those areas.

1. Run a current through the back of the heart chakra with your right hand and pull painful energy released by your client into your left hand. (There are many different techniques of moving energy but I'll just use this one now). Ask the person to contact the pain

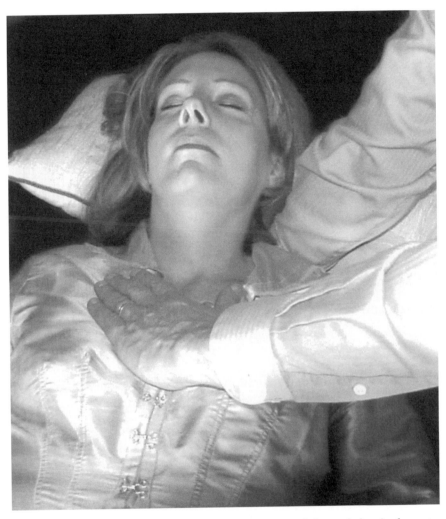

Place your left hand over the front of the person's heart chakra (in the center of the chest) and your right hand under their back on the other side of their heart chakra (slipped between the upper part of their shoulder and neck).

energetically, by getting them to focus on the feelings rather than particular situations. This bypasses the mind's tendency to analyze and tangle-up the flow of energy. Ask them to look through their body, see their heart lying there, torn to shreds, the way others left it when their heart was broken. Ask them to *feel* the pain that tore it apart, not only the pain that they've experienced before, but the pain they couldn't bear to feel. To feel the parts of those experiences filled with so much overwhelming terror, numbness and unconsciousness that they just refused to feel or even acknowledge when they first received them. When overwhelmed by pain, our body's tendency is to shut down and become unconscious. The trick is to get your client to feel it fully—*but just for a second or two*—which will allow their body to unlock and release it. Through personal observation, I've found that when someone grieves, the pain is released for about five or six seconds as it hovers above the heart chakra. If it isn't energetically removed, it will go back into the heart. This may account for why people who have lost spouses grieve for years with no apparent relief.

2. At that point, just pull it or scoop it out of them with your left hand and deposit it on the floor or into a plant, shaking out your hand when you're finished.

Warning: I DO NOT recommend that you pull negative energy into your own body. Scoop it out as described above and make sure that you clear yourself out fully after the session using one or more of the techniques described in Chapter 14.

3. Encourage them to give up the painful energy by exchanging it with lots of warm, loving energy which you're sending through the back of their heart with your right hand. This will bring about a profound sense of relief and healing. Do this gradually, asking them to pick up one piece of their poor, shredded heart at a time and squeeze out the pain, starting from present time and working backwards. Remind them to focus on the pain itself, rather than specific instances. As they do this they will feel "lumps" in the heart. Tell them that by feeling the pain, they will be able to release the pain contained within.

4. When this is accomplished, ask them to pick up the next piece and continue until every part of the pain has been felt, released and eliminated.

5. When the heart is completely drained of pain have them visualize taking a golden needle and golden thread made of love and ask them to sew the pieces, one by one, back together again. Ask them to watch as the loving energy that's now coming in from both of your hands is melding the pieces together, thus fixing that broken heart.

6. Have them visualize the energy filling their hearts, brimming over and up into their skull, bathing their brain, eyes, nose, cheeks, throat, ears, and tongue. Moving down their backs, shoulders and into their arms and fingers, through their chest, stomach, lower back, into their hips, thighs, legs and into their toes. Then have them visualize that love pouring out into their auric field, starting as a beautiful golden mist, moving a few feet out, surrounding their entire body. Feel it get thicker and thicker as it now serves as a filter, a filter made of love which will only allow love in—allowing them to keep their hearts open at all times, flowing love out to everyone they come into contact with. The resulting smile of relief and fulfillment is soon seen. No more broken heart!

The next step is to get them to forgive themselves and others as explained in Chapter 11 while running energy through their heart chakra. The resulting tears of joy will mark the beginning of a new life for that person—the one which they came here to fulfill.

A Reminder: Before attempting to fix their broken heart, make sure you first get rid of any fear the person is holding in their second chakra as well as any anger they're holding in their third. Once these negative emotions are released, you are also removing any reason the person has to prevent their heart from opening again.

Chapter 11

Managing Energy

Have you been abandoned, harmed or betrayed? It's a fact that, without your awareness, your energy is constantly flowing out to everyone who has betrayed or abandoned you. In our need to understand ourselves and be understood, we as beings, on a deep, energetic level, want those who have inflicted pain on us to feel what it's like to be in that position. When we focus our attention on revenge, or other destructive thoughts, we unconsciously allow our energy to stream out to everyone who has hurt us.

Do you really want others to continue getting your energy without asking for it? Here's what you can do about it right now. Close your eyes and look through your body as an "energy being." Locate a line of energy flowing out from you to a person who has harmed you. If you can't locate it, just imagine where it is in your body. More often than not the energy will originate from somewhere in the vicinity of your second chakra.

It's hard to acknowledge that sometimes the people who have hurt us the most in life are actually, in some way, our greatest teachers. The most beneficial lessons in life are sometimes the most painful. Have you located that line of energy? Good! When you're ready, I want you to cut it, but here's the hard part, do it with gratitude and appreciation, thanking that person for being your teacher. Now, pull back all of the energy that person has taken from you. It's your energy and it does what you tell it to do! Just use your intention—which is effortless. Have you done it? Open your eyes. Notice how you are feeling now.

It's an interesting paradox that you can more easily control many situations by letting go than by holding on. By letting go, you allow your intentions to work the way they are supposed to. Holding on ties up too much of your energy. Letting go frees it up to be used in a better way. Surrender is one way of letting go. Acceptance is another.

Raising Energy

When working with a client, the goal is to raise their emotional frequencies gradually, from numbness to fear; from anger to sadness; from pain to relief; from forgiveness, through hope, to love, compassion and joy; and on to make profound realizations. This moves them on their path toward achieving enlightenment. Their obvious relief and accompanying realizations place them in a frequency that they hadn't experienced in a long time—of which laughter and joy are reflections.

Trying to raise your energy level to a higher frequency through the use of a lower frequency such as despising some aspect of yourself is fruitless. This is because by focusing on that unwanted condition you're actually creating *more* of that condition. This is why dieting fails. By focusing on all that weight that you want to lose, you're creating more of it. You become what you think! By focusing your intentions on what you want to become and feeling that you've already achieved it, by engaging your creativity, imagination and emotions, you tap into an unlimited storehouse of energy. This will help you create the reality you desire.

Forgiveness

Another important lesson I've learned is that you can't love someone else if you don't love yourself. Forgiveness is the first step to self-healing. Forgiveness makes energy flow. Blame, shame, guilt, regret and judgment only clog it. More people come to me with an inability to love themselves than with any other problem. We all learn by our mistakes and there isn't anyone on this planet who is perfect. Ask yourself, is there something for which I can't forgive myself? Something over which you've been beating yourself up for years? If so, think of a close friend whom you love who isn't involved in any way with the incident you're feeling guilty about. Could you understand and forgive that person, whom you love, if he/she did the same thing? Of course you can! If you can forgive that person, why can't you forgive yourself? Are you that much better than everyone else? If not, why are you holding yourself up to a higher standard? It's true that as spirits we're all the same and we're all connected. We all make mistakes and those of us who make the most mistakes and learn from them go "back home" with more acquired wisdom than everyone else. Do yourself a favor, forgive yourself *right now* and start that energy flowing again.

Is there anyone whom *you* need to forgive? Take this opportunity and do it now! This may seem trite but all it takes is a simple decision. Holding onto a grudge only ties up and blocks your own energy and power. Think of forgiveness as a gift to yourself. By forgiving we don't have to forget. Forgetting might throw away the whole reason for the unpleasant experience—acquiring knowledge. Remembering eventually converts knowledge to wisdom, but forgiving is simply releasing energy from negatively affecting you.

Energy Vampires

There are people everywhere who can steal your energy. "Energy Vampires" is the popular term some healers use when referring to them. You can often tell when you've been "bitten" because after your contact with them has ended, you may feel exhausted, drained, nervous, tired, headachy, nauseous, dizzy or a host of other unpleasant feelings—each telling you that your energy has just been taken away.

Many years ago I worked as Art Director for a major TV network. I had dealings with three people over a considerable amount of time. Each time I went to see person "A," I'd get butterflies in my stomach. Person "B" would always give me a headache and person "C" would make me feel dizzy. This happened, consistently, each time I went to see each of them. My body was trying to tell me something—that they all were stealing my energy! Reflecting back now, I remember that their secretaries and other workers around them were always sick— further evidence of their self-serving energetic activities.

People "steal" energy because they've lost touch with their own source of it, which may be the earth or their personal connection with a Higher Power. In order to survive, they now rely upon obtaining it from others. Everything from losing an argument, being criticized, or engaging your sympathy, will leave you vulnerable to their "fangs." They may initiate arguments or find fault with others in an attempt to get attention. These, and other bad behaviors, may be the only way they received attention and energy from their parents as children. They may also get sick often to attract the attention of the "rescuers" out there who will come in, give them sympathy (and their own energy) and "save" them—at great personal expense.

When working on clients who are Energy Vampires I determine which connection they've lost. If it's their connection to the Earth that they've detached from I spend more time grounding them (re-connecting them and their energy to the earth) and clearing out their First Chakra. If it's their Seventh Chakra I find out what situation occurred in their lives to make them disconnect from their Higher Power—usually the death of someone close to them which they're now blaming their Source for having taken that person away from them.

By tuning in to what your body is telling you, you will know when someone is stealing your energy. You'll simply feel bad! On the other hand, there are people out there who make you feel wonderful. This is because they are giving you energy. Another reason why people go to healers! When you feel good about yourself you are also taking in energy. With energy work it is important, when giving, to develop the ability to pull and utilize energy from other sources (i.e. earth, nature, trees, ocean, wind, moon, universe, God, Goddess, etc.), and neither use your own, nor attempt to take away someone else's positive energy.

It's been my experience that when you do something to help yourself, such as distancing yourself from or closing the door entirely on those who drain you, the Universe rewards you by opening up a new door, bringing people and situations that are beneficial to you into your life. Before you are compensated, however, you first have to demonstrate your courage and willpower by making a decision and acting upon it. This can be a very rewarding leap of faith. Opening your fifth chakra can help you expedite this process significantly. It helps separate you from your "stuff" and you can see the "forest for the trees" again.

Like the painter who steps back from his canvas to view the entire perspective of his creation, opening up the fifth chakra can divert your attention from the narrow perspective that a day-to-day struggle for existence can bring. Your new perspective helps you to see the entire expanse of your life, and helps you gain insight into your reason for being here on this planet. As you start to get rid of your stuff, you may even begin to recover lost memories of early childhood and lifetimes past, which may provide a greater sense of your evolution as a spiritual being. Issues, which float around in your auric field, plus your own unwillingness to confront them, may be the main cause of not being able to remember your past.

Solving Problems

From an energy perspective, a problem is simply two impulses pushing or pulling us in opposite directions. Because this dilemma is actually a delicate balance of energy holding us suspended in indecision, all we have to do to dislodge it is to make a decision. This will make the energy flow one way or another. At that point, if you're listening, your intuition will kick in and tell you if it is the correct decision or not.

Remember, we all learn by our mistakes. Don't allow the fear of making them keep you from admitting your mistake and taking action to correct it by making a new decision. This adds to your knowledge and personal integrity. A flow of energy, even if it's going in the wrong direction, will be stronger than no flow at all. Energy can always be redirected.

"What the caterpillar calls the end,
the rest of the world calls a butterfly."
—Lao-tzu

Chapter 12

Past Lives

As with any subject from which you hope to benefit, it is necessary to be able to extract those parts that you can easily assimilate into your own experience and leave behind those that you cannot. I understand that for many people the subject of past lives does not fit into their present reality. It is, however, a part of my reality and therefore, I use that experience in my role as a healer.

I've found that once you start to clear out the heavy emotional charge—"stuff"—that surrounds and insulates your auric field, preventing you from remembering the past, your experiential memory tends to increase. There are some who can't remember their own childhood. This is an indication of emotional turmoil in that area. Healing sessions can gradually remove this trauma, sometimes enabling the person to recover and rehabilitate those long forgotten times. If you'd like to know more about this, there are many good books written on the subject (see resources listed at the end) or you can delve into your past with the help of a good Hypnotherapist or Past Life Regressionist.

It is my understanding that we each agree to take on a form of amnesia before coming here in order to keep the memories we had "back home" from interfering with our present lifetime—one which we chose to live and experience. It makes sense that if we knew the future we might be reluctant to go through some experiences that we agreed to undergo because those instances most often contain pain and loss. Each time we come back into a new life we learn about a different aspect of life, love and loss. It's true that sometimes we can't really appreciate what we have until we lose it. Life is something we all face losing eventually but it's important to know that our death here is our birth somewhere else. Each lifetime helps us acquire a bit more awareness and allows us to grow as a spirit.

Death and Reality

A while back I heard a story about a fellow who had received bad news from his doctor, telling him he was going to die. A short time thereafter he did. Later it was found that the diagnosis was incorrect and that this person had nothing wrong with him! Your spiritual component is far more powerful than your body.

Our energy system is constantly telling our bodies what to do, and to a large extent, we create our own reality based on the information with which we choose to agree. Once we make that agreement it becomes a goal or type of contract. We hand over our control to our belief system, which then acts to automatically focus our intentions, thoughts and energy on fulfilling that goal. Sometimes this, unfortunately, becomes our reality. There is probably nothing more debilitating to your energy system than someone in authority telling you that you're going to die! Fear has a devastating way of forcing us to give up and become helpless. It is designed to do that—to control you. Whether that person's information is correct or not, if you agree with it, you will die.

Lost hope is a life lost. I feel that it is my duty as a healer to offer my clients hope, regardless of what they've been told. My ultimate goal is to get them to calmly accept any outcome. If they can remove their focus and energy from the fear of dying (or other fears), that same energy can instead be applied to the possibility of fixing the problem.

Think of our physical universe as a three-dimensional canvas, on which we paint our energy—directed by our thoughts and intentions. The fantastic miracles of life, which surround us every day, are all by-products of that creation. If you can change the direction of a person's intention, thoughts, and outlook, which are all energy, it is possible to change their outcome. If, however, you don't have a goal, no goal will ever be realized.

The one certainty we all have in this life is that we will all eventually die. None of us can say, with total assurance, just how long each of us has on this planet. Someone with a terminal illness, for example, can easily outlive someone else in seemingly perfect health. About three years ago, a client with colon and liver cancer came to see me. The colon cancer had been removed in an operation but the cancer had spread to his liver. His doctor was emphatic in telling him that the metastices in his liver would not go away. I shrunk them energetically on his first visit. When he went to get an MRI the following week, they were completely gone! His doctor, very puzzled and apparently frustrated, told him "Don't worry, they'll come back!" None of his cancer has returned.

It's interesting to note that as you handle and resolve the issues that cause the dis-ease in the first place, there is often no reason for it to reappear. It is important to recognize, that this dis-ease usually forces the person to take a hard look at their life and their reason for being on this planet at this time.

When a person's outlook goes below a certain threshold, usually over an extended time, that person will unconsciously make choices that will eventually do their body in. Smoking and drinking to excess are examples. Obviously those considering the subject of suicide have lost any sight or hope of regaining the quality and dignity of life they once enjoyed. The pain and feeling of hopelessness, understandably, can be overwhelming. Providing immediate relief in a healing session to help them rise above that threshold is imperative. An instant referral to a good therapist or psychiatrist is also crucial.

Time and space are illusions and are perceived differently by different people, based on individual perspective. In some cases an hour can seem like ten years, and at other times ten years can pass by in a flash. Just maybe, things will change. Adapting to that change is a challenge, but within that challenge lies hope and a great opportunity. A hope that circumstances will eventually change. And an opportunity to do things differently, take on a different perspective, and allow joy, relaxation and love to enter and nurture your life. Your situation has a definite possibility of transformation.

Dis-ease may create the opportunity for you to discover the reason for being here now and could motivate you to accomplish and fulfill your true purpose in life. It might even be something as simple as learning to give and receive love on different levels. In the end, it's not how many years you have on this planet but the quality of your relationships and the love conveyed as a result of that experience. Love is truly what we're made of and, once given, it is the gift that will endure throughout eternity. Once received, it is yours to keep forever.

Don't Get Attached

A healing session is probably one of the most intimate experiences a healer and client will ever have. You are linking spiritually with each other. As beings, we long for a spiritual union with our Source.

After having asked to witness creation during a meditation several years ago, I was given the following vision. A huge, golden liquid sun made of love appeared. Droplets were formed, coming from those magnificent rays of seemingly liquid light. These droplets became individual, glowing "baby" spirits. I was shown that each of us, in a sense, is a piece of the Divine, but we are now separated from our source, which creates our need to be reunited.

When we recognize that piece of God in others, in a spiritual sense, our natural desire is to merge with it. This sometimes motivates us to connect with another on a deep spiritual, emotional or physical level. It's a step closer towards being whole again! Attractions on every level can result from this phenomenon. We often search outside ourselves in order to fulfill that feeling of completeness, in the end realizing that what we were searching for was inside all along. This realization has made it easier for me to discover and love that divinity in myself and not look so hard to find it elsewhere.

This intense connection is what attracts and links us as beings on every level. Don't, however, confuse this feeling of unconditional love, which flows through you when doing a healing, with other feelings such as romance. Feelings that intense are sometimes difficult to distinguish, for both the healer and the client. As a healer, it is personally validating to know that the unconditional love you are feeling, as it passes through you, is reaching and healing your client. But it is imperative that you realize the sacredness of this temporary spiritual union, your purpose as a healer, and your responsibility as a facilitator to guide your clients on their way to greater personal insights and a higher awareness as they continue to fulfill their life's purpose.

Opening a person's heart for the first time in many years might sometimes enable them to experience overwhelming euphoric feelings which they had long since left for dead, and in the process they might feel, more acutely, the lack of love in their own lives. That realization might be accompanied by a great deal of sadness as they realize that they have been ignoring their present relationships and their willingness to work at having more love in their lives. As a result they might become attached to you in an intense way, since you are now a source of that love, maybe the only source. This attention can be very flattering, but developing the discipline to maintain professional boundaries and keeping your own personal needs out of the session is necessary.

I often feel like a gatekeeper, in a sense, helping people through the door and up the stairs to a better life. Once they are free of their "stuff" and out of sight, they are off to encounter new challenges. They resume living their own lives, which is as it should be. New people have often entered my life at a time when they were at a crossroads in their own. I recognize that this was not a coincidence. It is understandable to get attached to people with whom you so closely work. Sharing and letting go of your pain with someone whom you trust is a sacred experience. Going through life and death situations with someone, for instance, is especially bonding. Being able to let go, regardless of the outcome, is also an important quality that we all must acquire as healers. If you truly love someone unconditionally, you will want what's best for that person, even if it feels like a huge loss to you. Sometimes our clients die and we grieve for them like any other close friend. We must, however, shed that grief and get back to work. Don't look at death as a sign that you've failed—you haven't! Whether a client lives or dies is not up to you. We can't possibly know what is in their best spiritual interests, nor can we control the outcome. Maybe it was their time to leave. Maybe it's exactly what they, as a spirit, planned, having completed every task they came here to do. Try to look at it as a brand new start for the person somewhere else.

We each have our own personal views on life and death. Be careful not to impose yours on anyone else. Treat everyone with the same love, respect, courtesy, and consideration that you would like to receive and that's how you'll be treated.

Even though I frequently offer to be there for my clients as a friend as well as a healer, the reality is that once they have completed that which they came to me to work out and resolve, they are off to continue on their own unique path. Some of my saddest personal moments have been watching these friends leave. But it's helped me realize that as you continue to understand your true purpose for being here, your Source will always bring you someone new to take their place—someone whom you can help through that magical door, and on their way to a better life. Many will eventually pass through, so when they arrive, greet them like the old friends they soon will be, and you will have another opportunity to fulfill your reason for being here.

There is no easier way to find your "soul-mates" than by being on a spiritual path. A select few of these special beings may remain in your life for the duration and beyond, sometimes as close friends, sometimes as extraordinary spiritual partners, who will share your life, nurture and honor you, as you do them. In the end, we will all reach the same destination, and together will celebrate the trials and tribulations that we went through and overcame, back down on that tiny little planet called Earth.

Chapter 13

Distance Healing

Once you've been practicing running energy on people, sending it out to others from a distance can be relatively easy. The reason that you can affect change on someone else at a great distance, or even just across the room, is that we are all connected as spirits and so the distance we perceive in a physical sense is an illusion. Spending a lifetime as a spirit in a body can make you profoundly believe that illusion. You are a very powerful being, capable of doing many unusual, wonderful things and sending energy to someone else is just one more way of utilizing your innate abilities. It is another way of reaffirming and strengthening the connection that is already there.

Even if the person is unaware that you're sending them energy, it will have a positive effect on them, provided they are not closed off to it. Their higher self, the part of their spirit that knows their true purpose in life—and is dedicated to fulfilling that purpose, is aware of such subtle changes and will make the decision at that level when the time is right. Sometimes people who are dying in a hospital have already decided that they want to die. At that point, when you send them energy they will either refuse it, or take it and use it to get out of their body and leave—often at the exact time you are sending it.

A while ago I was asked to do hands-on work on an elderly woman with cancer by her daughter who was a friend of mine. The woman told her daughter that she wanted to live. But as soon as she got me alone, she confided to me that her deceased husband was waiting for her "in heaven" and that she wanted to join him but didn't want to upset her daughter by telling her.

On another occasion, my friend Peg, a social worker, hired me to do a distance healing on her mother, who was dying in a hospital far away. That night I tuned in to her mom, got a clear picture in my mind of her lying in a hospital bed, and started to send her energy. I felt it bounce back and visually saw her mom with her palms facing me as if to say, "No, I don't want it." I called Peg the next day and told her, "I can't take your money because your mom doesn't want the energy." She responded saying, "That's just like my mother!"

When energy is refused, it will feel to you just like the kind of rejection you got from someone as a teenager. You'll probably feel a little inadequate and feel the energy bouncing back at you. A healer friend once told me that when she sends someone energy and it is refused, she just packs it up in a little box with a ribbon around it. She then leaves it at the feet of the person, with a gift card stating it's theirs to use at any time he/she chooses, over the next thousand years.

Some people, even though they've decided to leave, may change their minds after absorbing the love sent and decide to use it to hang around a little longer or get better in a miraculous way. This is *their* decision, not yours. Your intention, as well as theirs, makes this scenario possible. Your ability to send and manipulate energy is limited only by your own intention, your ability to feel and send this love, and the other person's acceptance of it. Please remind yourself that even though we each have a piece of God inside of us, it's not up to us to play God. Our client makes the ultimate decision to stay or leave. It is not up to us and should have no bearing on how good a healer we are perceived to be by others or ourselves.

Clients sometimes come to me with a specific condition to heal, but will leave my session with the condition apparently unchanged. Another more important aspect of themselves may be remedied instead—something which they may only notice sometime later. Regardless of whether you're doing hands-on or distance healing, it's important to acknowledge that we don't always know the actual reason for their dis-ease—even if it seems apparent. Always treat the entire being and not just the current ailment or body part. We are all growing on many levels at one time. By not limiting our scope of healing to a specific condition, we are honoring the spirit's reason for that condition in its evolutionary journey through time.

Simple is Best

There are as many techniques to achieve distance healing as there are to doing hands-on healing. They vary from teacher to teacher, school to school. Simple is best. If you understand the true essence of energy, you can easily develop your own methods and techniques of working. I am giving you the basics so that you will gain a sense of accomplishment very quickly as you set up the rituals and techniques that will feel comfortable and make sense to you. The repetition and practice will soon have you doing distance work naturally, without attention to complicated techniques. Let your intuition help you discover what works best for you.

Clearing Out & Tuning In

1. Sit in a chair with your feet flat on the floor, palms on thighs facing up, relaxing the entire body as you take in a few deep breaths. Send your roots down through the floor deep into the earth while pulling up energy into your body. Move it all the way through your body, out of the top of your head to the heavens as you connect with your Source. Give thanks for being able to be used as an instrument of healing.

2. Ask for protection for yourself and the person you are working on. Breathe in loving energy, filling yourself and the room with this tranquility and peace. A few ways in which I practice are by sending my energy to the person; using my "energy body" to travel to the person; or by asking the person's "energy body" be brought to me to work on. Let's try the first for now:

3. Visualize the person in your mind's eye—even if you've never met them before. Ask your Source that the person be healed unconditionally. Don't limit your request, just send energy out for the highest good so that anything that needs to be healed, will.

4. Start pulling in energy from the earth, up into your heart and down your arms. Now connect with your Source and feel that energy coming in from above, through your head, into your heart, down your arms and out of your hands. If you prefer, it can also be sent out of your heart.

5. Visualize the person whom you are working on and where they are at that moment (home, hospital bed, etc.). Get in touch with that person by feeling their feelings. You may pick up their sadness, depression, pain, and often hopelessness.

6. Surround them in the bright white light of this healing energy. See it go into them, and watch their demeanor change gradually as you flow it into them. Get into their body if they allow you to, and see out of their eyes. Picture dark clouds surrounding them. See your own light parting the clouds, entering their eyes, filling them with warmth, joy and hope. See the clouds slowly parting, letting in more nurturing light. Feel their emotions change from sad to hopeful as you fill their bodies and auric fields with lots of loving light. Start to hear joyful noises (birds chirping, children playing) and know that they can hear them too.

7. When you're done, send them a last burst of energy and start to pull back. Thank your Source for the energy and for having healed them. Convey gratitude for allowing you to be used as a healing instrument. Thank the person for allowing you to work on him/her. Slowly withdraw, leaving the connection with your Source still feeding them. Know deep inside that what you just participated in actually happened.

Remember that you are acting as a conduit and that you should only be sending energies which you are pulling from other sources, *not* your own. If you give away your own energy, you stand the risk of becoming extremely drained, energetically.

My Father

Sometimes distance healing can help a person to ease the transition from one world to another. One personal example was when my father was dying in a hospital, about five hours away. Week after week, members of my family kept holding onto him, pleading with him to stay even though it was apparent to me, and most everyone else, that he was ready to leave. Not wanting to disappoint, he endured. After continually being frustrated by his spiritual dilemma, I did a distance healing on him. By getting in touch with him on a spiritual level, I sent him a ton of energy, telling him that he had done everything he needed to do in this lifetime and that it was OK to leave. I assured him that we would see him again and that Mom was waiting for him. I flooded him with lots of loving energy, took in a deep breath, sent it to him, felt him separate from his body, and ended the session. Twenty minutes later I got a call from my sister who told me that she was with him twenty minutes before—when he died. She described his passing as peaceful. She said, "He took in one last deep breath and left."

Using Photos

You can also use a photo of the person to help you visualize. While visiting my son at college in upstate New York, I happened to enter a store in town and overheard the owner telling a friend how worried she was about her daughter, who was far away at a college in Long Island, had the flu and wasn't getting better. She had tried all sorts of herbal and homeopathic remedies with no success. I approached her, letting her know that I couldn't help overhearing the circumstances of her distress and introduced myself as a healer. She pointed to a photo of her daughter on a bulletin board behind her, I asked if it would be OK with her if I sent her energy. She agreed, as she looked on with amusement while helping the next customer.

I placed my hands over the photo and sent energy to her for about five minutes then proceeded to look around her fascinating shop for the next several minutes as she finished helping the remaining customers. We then started to talk about healing and I thanked her for allowing me to send her daughter energy. Very curious, she asked me to wait as she picked up the phone, called her daughter and asked how she was feeling. Her daughter responded, "I've been feeling *much* better these last ten minutes and the fever has gone away!" Since then, I have been invited to teach my healing workshops in the back of her store whenever I come to her town for a visit. Remember that you can do this too!

*"The torment of precautions
often exceeds the dangers to be avoided."
—Napoleon Bonaparte*

Chapter 14

Self Healing

Running energy on yourself can help you immensely when healing a cut, scrape, burn, or a broken bone—once it's set. By placing your hand on the affected area of a cut, for instance, and running energy through it, it is possible to get the blood to coagulate and stop bleeding very quickly.

I was sharing a glass of wine with a writer friend as she dropped her glass, which shattered all over the floor. As we were picking up the pieces, a shard got stuck in her finger. We got it out and I wrapped my hand around her bleeding finger. Within about thirty seconds it stopped completely and was unnoticeable thereafter. I've applied this principle to everything from cut fingers to bloody noses. Energy work can have a positive effect on insect bites, such as bee stings, as well. The key is to apply the energy as soon after the injury has occurred to circumvent the body's defensive tendency to make the area swell.

Running energy can work on almost everything, including the common cold. I find situations that take the average person 7 –10 days to recover, I can usually get through in three. However, when you're feeling *very* sick and totally depleted, self-healing is like trying to jump-start your car with a dead battery. This is when you need to be in the presence of another healer, or healers, with a stronger electromagnetic field to get that energy flowing again and recharge your battery. Sometimes that requires getting more than one person to work on you simultaneously. This energy will assist any medications you've taken—even chicken soup—to work better. You will also find that running energy works on plants and animals. They both love it! Whenever I go to someone's home to do a healing, the animals will park themselves very near the person on which I'm working—within the auric fields of myself and my client. They can feel the energy! Usually it will feel so comfortable that they'll fall asleep.

Clearing Out Negativity from Yourself

We all pick up other people's "stuff" from time to time. It's a normal occurrence, a by-product of our compassion and empathy. The more sensitive we are, the more of this stuff we accumulate. Regardless of whether it's our own or someone else's, it's important to know how to get rid of it. Here are a few suggestions:

Energy Shower: When taking a shower in the morning I sometimes visualize that pure, clean water passing through the top of my head, moving through my entire body, washing away and dissolving all the tension, worries, problems, and everything else. I watch it as it pours out of me and down the drain, feeling my energy return.

Recharging Bath: Pour a box of baking soda into a warm bath and soak in it for a while. It will clear out your Auric Field and body's energy system.

Revitalizing Drink: Drink lots of water. Water attaches itself to our negative "stuff" and helps us purify our bodies.

Energy Shake: You can violently shake out your hands, arms and the rest of your body, the way a dog shakes off moisture after having had a swim. Dancing has the same effect!

Breathe it out: You can also take in huge breaths, hold them and while intentionally attaching your negative energy to that breath, very forcefully breathe it out, expelling the negative energy.

Ground it: If sitting down, on a chair, keep your feet on the floor and pull red earth energy up through your entire body, down your arms, out of your hands and into the seat of your chair, with the intention of grounding it deep into the earth. The current going through you will take with it any negative energies accumulated in your body.

Stamp it: While walking, stamp your feet on the ground and as you do, intentionally force energy out of your body and into the earth.

Rake it: If you're with a partner, you can take turns elongating your "energy fingers" and raking them through your partner's entire body, like a comb through hair, then shaking out your hands and fingers to remove the excess energy.

Sage it: Burning white sage (available in almost any New Age or Native American store), also called "smudging," helps dissipate negative energy and leaves the area with a unique but clean smell.

Try coming up with some "energy clearing" methods of your own! Just remember that everything is energy and your intention is moving it. Allow your imagination and intuition to guide you.

Using Affirmations

Words are energy. When we tell ourselves anything (even when talking to ourselves) we are giving instructions to our mind to create that reality. Affirmations are formulated sentences, repeated over and over again, in an attempt to program our sub-conscious minds to create a new or different reality. Here are some helpful guidelines to follow when using them:

Present tense: It's important to speak our affirmations in the present tense. Such as "I am joyful and happy with every aspect of my life." If you were to say, "I will be joyful and happy" you are helping your sub-conscious mind create the picture that you *will* be in the future, but not at the present time. And since we are always in present time, that future may never arrive.

Be positive: State your affirmations in a positive way. Our subconscious minds are full of pictures and they don't have pictures for "not," "don't" and other negatives. If I say "Don't think of chocolate." That's exactly what I'm going to think of! Create an affirmation such as, "Today is a beautiful day" rather than "It's not going to rain today." This way you're giving energy to what you want rather than what you don't!

Be specific: State exactly what you want and you'll have a better chance of getting it. Don't be vague or generalize.

Action follows thought. There is a lot of power in what we think. If you become truly aware of your thoughts, from moment to moment, this will give you a good indication of where your energy is going and what it is creating. Remember that your intention directs your thoughts. Start using your intentions to direct your life and see where it takes you

*"If you are distressed by anything external,
the pain is not due to the thing itself
but to your own estimate of it;
and this you have the power to revoke
at any moment."*
—Marcus Aurelius

Chapter 15

Guided Visualizations

In order to assist you in understanding how you might be able to utilize energy more effeciently, I'd like to take you on a little journey into exploring and becoming familiar with your own energy.

You may have a friend read the following to you or, if you are alone, read it into a tape recorder and play it back. If a tape recorder isn't handy just read each point and meditate on it for a few seconds. Find a comfortable spot. Relax by taking in a few deep breaths, and begin.

Everything is Energy Visualization:

- Breathe in the future, breathe out the past. With each breath you take you are becoming more and more relaxed and at ease.

- Take a moment to just feel your body.

- Start to feel all the tension you've accumulated in your body.

- Be aware of where you are holding it.

- Gradually start letting go of all the "stuff" you've accumulated in recent memory. Let go of every aggravation, frustration, annoyance, worry, fear, concern, loss. Everything! Just watch them lift and float away.

- Just for now, I'd like you to forget everything you've been taught about medicine and healing.

- Imagine that you and everything around you is composed of energy.

- Imagine waves of energy that are as vital to you as the air you breathe, flowing through you, around you and into all living things, giving them life.

- Feel this energy keeping your body and mind alive and healthy.

- Feel that subtle energy moving inside your body.

- Feel your luminous radiation moving outside your body helping you to interact with your external environment.

- Picture an electromagnetic field made up of this energy surrounding your body. It's your aura.

- See your body as a creation of this auric field, rather than assuming that this auric field is a by-product of your body.

- Imagine what happens to your energy when you get angry with someone or when someone hurts you.

- Feel the movement of this energy diminish when you begin to take life too seriously.

- Think of a loss, and feel your energy constricting. Now feel more loss being pulled towards you as a result of your own energy resonating in that frequency.

- Think of something which brings joy into your life and feel your energy expanding, now notice more joy being attracted to you magnetically because of this new wavelength which you are now resonating.

- Imagine the flow of your energy increasing, becoming more fluid and extending outward when you laugh.

- Thought is energy and your thoughts give your energy movement.

- Think of something you fear and notice how your thoughts are giving greater energy and importance to that fear.

- Feel your spirit contract when you mistrust your deepest feelings. Feel your spirit expand when you validate your own ability to know.

- Recall a fragrance, which brings back good memories, and note how these pictures in your mind are made up of energy.

- Imagine a blockage of energy occurring in yourself whenever an emotional issue is triggered and not dealt with, preventing this vital energy from being absorbed and utilized by your body.

- Imagine an abundance of energy flowing through you whenever one of your issues is resolved.

- Now think of someone whom you dislike. Feel your own energy draining as a result of *your* decision to dislike that person.

- Think of someone who loves you and feel your energy growing as a result of their love.

- Feel your energy go out to someone whom *you* love.

- Smile, and notice how your smile opens up your own heart. Remember how in the past, your smile has opened the hearts of others.

- Focus on feeling acceptance for everyone in your life.

- Start to think of everything and everyone whom you are grateful for.

- Feel that energy expand out to everything around you.

- Feel your energy harmonizing with Nature.

- Allow your spirit to view your surroundings and absorb the beauty in everything you see.

- Feel your connection to everyone you love.

- Send out thankful energy to the Universe.

- Feel the love all around you.

- Allow that love to permeate your heart, body and soul.

- Feel the vibration of your own energy.

- Tune in to your Source of divine energy.

- Feel the magnificent, loving, vibrational quality of your Source's energy.

- Notice how it calms you and makes you feel that all is well.

- Match all of your own feelings to that higher frequency of energy.

- Feel your connection to all things.

- Feel the love inside and outside of you.

- Know that you *are* love.

- Take in a deep breath and slowly open your eyes, reacquainting yourself with the room.

Layers Guided Visualization:

I've had great successes in doing this simple visualization with my clients. Many of them have never been the same again—nor would they want to be!

Close your eyes and very gently, start taking in some deep breaths. But I want you to picture yourself taking them in through the bottoms of your feet, filling up your body. Then breathing out through the bottoms of your feet.

With each breath you take, I want you to feel yourself getting more and more relaxed. Breathe in relaxation, breathe out all the "stuff" that tends to stick to your body, making you not feel well—problems, worries, concerns, fears, pains, aggravations, frustrations, annoyances, anger, losses, threatened losses—all that stuff.

Breathe out the past and breathe in the future, a bright wonderful future of your own creation.

Feel your body lying there being gently pulled lower and lower by gravity.

Feel your stomach expanding and contracting as you breathe.

Feel your heart beating.

Feel my fingers touching your feet.

Feel your blood coursing through your veins, moving throughout your body.

Feel the weight of your clothing pressing on your body.

Feel every part of your body surrendering to gravity.

Feel those subtle energies moving inside and outside your body giving you life and allowing you to be here with me today—and I'm very honored to have you here.

Get in touch with your body. I want you to give it permission to do something that you might not have done so far this lifetime. Give it permission to let go of all the "stuff" you've accumulated in your body.

I want you to get in touch with your body now and give it permission to let go and release the last month's worth of accumulated "stuff." Let go of all the problems, worries, concerns, fears, pains, aggravations, frustrations, annoyances, anger, losses, threatened losses. Feel them unlocking from every part of you, detaching and peeling off you like a layer of skin that you no longer need or want, floating upwards, moving farther and farther out into the distance as you watch them dissolve into the universe, leaving you lighter, more relaxed and at ease.

Note: As you're doing this visualization in session with your client, you're actually starting at the person's feet and gently peeling their stuff from their auric field all the way up to their head, with each layer.

I want you to get even deeper into your body now—closer in communication with it. I want you to give your body permission to unlock and release all of that stuff which you've accumulated over the past year. Feel them unlocking from every part of you, detaching and again just peeling off of you like another layer of skin that you no longer need or want, floating upwards, moving farther and farther out into the distance as you watch them dissolve into the universe, leaving you even lighter, more relaxed, more at ease.

Your body's been waiting a long time for you to give it permission to let go of that stuff—as we all hold onto our own stuff. We blame others for it. It gives us our "victim" status, justifying our attacks on others but actually we are responsible for holding onto it. And when you give your body permission to let go of that stuff, your body is overjoyed because that is where you hold it. You exert an great deal of your body's energy just holding onto it.

I want you to get even deeper into your body now—closer in communication with it. I want you to give your body permission to unlock and release the last ten years of accumulated stuff. Feel it unlocking from every part of you, detaching and again just peeling off of you like another layer of skin that you no longer want, floating upwards, moving farther and farther out into the distance as you watch it dissolve into the universe, leaving you even lighter, more relaxed, more at ease.

I want you to get even deeper into your body now—even closer in communication with it. And I want you to give your body permission to unlock and release all the stuff you've accumulated throughout the last half of your life. Feel it unlocking from every part of you, detaching and again just peeling off of you like another layer of skin you no longer want, floating upwards, moving farther and farther out into the distance as you watch it dissolve into the universe, leaving you even lighter, more relaxed, more at ease.

Now I want you to get as deep into your body as you can and closely in communication with every single cell. And I want you to give your body total permission to unlock and release *everything* you've accumulated since before birth. Every problem, every concern, every worry, every fear, all the pain, frustrations, and annoyances of life, all the anger, losses, threatened losses—everything! Feel them all unlocking, detaching, and peeling off of you like another layer of skin that you will never have any use for again, floating upwards, moving farther and farther out into the distance as you watch them dissolve into the universe, leaving you even lighter, more relaxed, and completely at ease.

Now I want you to give your body permission to do one more thing. Reverse the magnetic charge, that has held that stuff there for so long, so that at any time in the future, when confronted by more of that stuff, it will be repelled by your body and not held there. Give your body permission to reverse that charge *now*!

The Ultimate Relaxation Visualization:

Note: This visualization immediately follows the one preceeding. As you're doing this exercise with your client, you are putting your hands above the areas I'm describing and energizing those areas as you pull off any excess "stuff" which you encounter. I have also discovered that the more relaxed a person is, the easier it is for them to absorb the energy that you're sending.

Locate where you are in your body right now. Bring your complete consciousness all the way through your body, down to your toes and command that area to completely relax and let go. Tell every muscle, every bone, every fiber, every nerve, every cell to just relax and let go.

Now I want you to move your consciousness up to your ankles and simply command that area to completely relax and let go. Your body does what you tell it to do so expect it to comply.

Move your consciousness up through your calves to your knees, again, gently commanding that area to relax and let go.

Note: You're again energetically pulling off any excess tension from that part of the person's auric field which you are working on, enabling them to get into a deeper state of relaxation.

Now move your consciousness from your knees up to your thighs, hips, intestines, all the way around to the buttocks, and again just command that area to relax and let go. No effort is necessary, just your intention which is effortless. Feel every cell surrendering to gravity.

Move your consciousness all the way up through your spine to your kidneys, stomach, pancreas, liver, gallbladder, spleen, diaphragm—all the organs in the center of your body. Tell them to gently relax and let go.

Move through your heart, your lungs, up to your shoulders and around to your back. Command this area to completely relax and let go.

Move your consciousness down your shoulders, down your arms to your elbows, and all the way down to your hands and fingers, telling them all to relax and let go.

Move your consciousness up through your neck, feel your lower jaw, tongue and throat gently relaxing. Move up through your eyes, through your sinus cavities and ear canals, all the way through your skull to your brain, to every hair on your head, gently commanding every part of you to completely relax and let go.

Melting Visualization

Note: This immediately follows the previous visualization.

I want you to now look through your body to the center, the stomach area, and I want you to spot a bright spinning sun located in this area. If you can't see it, just imagine it. I want you to watch it as it spins around, sending beautiful, warm rays of golden, glittery light dancing out in every direction as it spins.

It's getting larger as it spins, radiating throughout the insides of your body, filling you with feelings of warmth, caring, nurturing and love.

You're watching as it gets larger and starts to rise up out of your body, gently floating to the ceiling, beating down on every part of you, filling you with warmth all over.

Now, the light from this sun has special properties, for as this light touches the cells in your body, your cells respond by melting away, melting into the table.

Your entire DNA and molecular structure are decomposing. Allow them to do so.

You are feeling a little like an ice sculpture on a hot summer's day at the beach, as you melt into the table. Completely dissolving and becoming weightless, being pulled by gravity, lower and lower into the table, now through the table, now you're beneath the table, gently floating to the floor.

You're moving through the floorboards, and into the foundation of this building going lower and lower.

You're now surrounded by dark, rich soil, which you can smell, taste and feel all around you. You are absorbing all those life-giving nutrients into your being. These are the same properties that have given life to everything on this planet, and now they are being offered to you as a gift from Mother Earth. Accept this gift and feel yourself growing as a being, getting larger and larger, fortifying you for the rest of your life.

You're being pulled by gravity now, lower and lower through sand, gravel and rock formations. The earth is starting to act like a huge filter, filtering out all the unwanted emotional baggage you no longer need or want. Think of this baggage as clothing in your attic that you've kept around your entire lifetime, expecting to wear it again. But this stuff doesn't even fit anymore! Get rid of it! Lighten your load!

Cast this baggage off as you go lower and lower, watching as the earth gladly takes them away—lightening your load. The lower you go, the more safe and secure you are feeling. The earth is taking care of you and is protecting you.

As you go lower you are starting to feel a connection to all the living things on the planet above you. To the grasses, the trees, flowers, animals, and to all the billions and billions of people high above you.

You can feel the vibrations from the huge oceans as their waves are crashing against the shoreline. You can feel a connection to the huge mountain ranges high above them and the sky above them. All is one— and you're part of it. And it feels so wonderful to be such an integral part of something so huge and magnificent!

You're moving deeper and deeper into the earth casting off more and more pieces of that baggage you no longer need or want and you're entering an underground stream which is bathing you and cleansing you and taking away all of the impurities of your life. Allow it to wash through you completely making you feel so clean.

As you go deeper and deeper into the earth, you're casting off more and more of that baggage you no longer need. It's getting warmer as you go lower, through the various parts of the earth's mantle, closer and closer to the center of the earth. You can see that hot molten lava ahead but it doesn't burn, it feels soothing as you pull that energy into your being, glowing in a beautiful orange glow. You're filling up with that glorious energy and feel yourself getting as large as a hot air balloon.

This may be the first time you've re-charged your battery in this manner since before you were born. It's time.

You are establishing this connection with the Earth, which can't be broken. You can call upon it at any time for more energy and it will comply immediately.

You're starting to move upward again, through that huge filter we call the earth, casting off the remaining vestiges of that baggage you no longer need or want. Get rid of it all and lighten your load! That energy from the center of the earth is following you now as you ascend through various parts of the earth's mantle.

You're entering a crystal cavern and are surrounded by thousands of beautiful quartz crystals all around you, each glistening in its own beautiful blue-green healing light, an energy that is now being absorbed by you—which will protect you in the future. Whenever you're feeling ill just remember it and its soothing light will ease your pain.

You're moving higher and higher up towards the surface, back through various rock formations, gravel and sand and you're back into that rich soil. You're being given another opportunity as a much larger being to absorb even more of those life-giving nutrients and properties as a gift from Mother Earth. You are fortifying yourself for the rest of your existence!

You're looking up and seeing the foundation of this building above you. You're moving up to it and through it, coming up through the floor here and you're at the base of your feet.

I want you to watch as the bottoms of your feet are opening and I want you to take that energy you've been pulling from the center of the earth and send it into the bottoms of your feet and watch as your bones are acting like huge sponges, glowing in a beautiful orange radiance as a result.

Note: *(Start to rub the soles of their feet in a circular motion).*

I'd like you to get back into your body through the bottoms of your feet to direct that energy from the center of the earth through your ankles, knees, thighs, and hips. Your kidneys and intestines are filling with that warm glowing energy.

Your spine is now glowing, one vertebrae at a time, creating lots of space in between each one. Your stomach, pancreas, diaphragm, liver, spleen, and gallbladder are all glowing now. Your heart is filling up and pumping that wonderful energy to every nerve in your system, calming you and making you feel so serene and relaxed! Your lungs are filling with it and are breathing that energy throughout your body as it moves up to your shoulders and surges down your arms and into your fingertips, which are now tingling as a result.

It's moving up your neck and into your skull through your brain, which is now glowing—as are your eyes, nose, cheeks, ears and tongue. Your hair is glistening with this energy and every single cell in your body is filling with this energy and is glowing in that beautiful orange glow.

The top of your head is opening, and out of it is pouring a geyser of lights, thousands of different colors pouring all over the room, bathing your body. You are feeling so light and are letting go of everything as you start to float out of the top of your head, gently rising to the ceiling.

You are moving through the ceiling, through the attic and the roof and you're out! Rising rapidly above the houses and trees, the cold air passing through you doesn't chill but instead feels invigorating as you go soaring higher and higher! You're letting go of everything, completely protected, feeling so free and liberated.

You can see the cars on the roadways and the neighboring towns as you ascend ever more rapidly. Up, up to the clouds! Through the clouds as you feel that thick moisture moving through you. You're flying freely above the clouds now and the sun is shining brightly through you. You're moving very rapidly way out to the edge of the atmosphere.

You're now moving beyond the atmosphere and are looking back at that big beautiful planet you left behind, in all of its glory, floating there in space, surrounded by blue and purple haze and looking so magnificent. No wonder why we love it so much—it's so beautiful!

You're moving beyond the earth now. As it gets smaller and smaller, you are soon surrounded by darkness but the darkness doesn't last, it's being replaced by billions and billions of twinkling stars. Stars that are welcoming you to a familiar place. A place where you feel you've been before.

As you're getting acclimated to this place you're starting to see some familiar looking figures in the distance, coming closer. And as they are approaching you, you're starting to recognize the smiles on their faces and the tears in their eyes—they're so happy to see you. Friends and family members who have passed on are coming for a visit!

As they approach you they are throwing their arms around you, hugging and kissing you and telling you how much they've missed you. Feel their energy. They are right there. You are right there! Listen to what they are telling you.

Your spirit guides are now coming from behind you around to the front. These beautiful angelic beings of light are telling you that they have been with you since your beginning and have been with you throughout all of your lifetimes. Listen to what they are telling you. They are saying that you are never alone, even when you're feeling that terrible emptiness and loneliness inside, they are always around you and always will be—for however many lifetimes it takes.

You're now starting to feel the presence of a much, much larger being. Its brilliant, bright white light is unmistakable as it totally permeates your being, filling you with complete unconditional love. Fill up with this love and as you do you are being given secrets concerning this love. You are being told that this is healing energy and that with it you can heal anyone you want back down on that little planet you just came from. And if you want more of that energy, all you have to do is simply give it away, and it will be replenished immediately by your source, and your own capacity to hold it will increase. So the more of this love you give, the more you will get. There is no limit to how many people you can give it to or how large a being you can become, filled with this love.

Now try it out. Think of someone on that little planet where you just came from who needs a healing, send that love out of your heart and watch it stream down to that planet, enveloping that person and watch that person smile as a result. You've just healed them! Notice that as soon as you did, that energy was being replenished by your Source. Only your own capacity to hold it has increased. Again, there's no limit to how many people you can give this love to and no limit to how much you can hold as a result. The more love you give, the more you will get!

You're establishing this connection with your Source, which can't be broken. You can call upon it at any time and it will comply immediately. As with energy, whenever you send it in any direction, you are pulled in that direction, which is what's happening now. As you start to travel back down to the planet, your friends and family are saying, "Goodbye for now, we love you! We're only a thought away!"

You're moving more rapidly towards the Earth, which is getting larger and larger as you approach it. You're moving down, down to the clouds, down through the clouds and beneath the clouds, zeroing in on the area where you came from. You see cars on the roadways, houses and trees and spot the rooftop where you exited. Moving down to it, now through it, through the attic, the attic floor, through the ceiling here and you're back, floating above your body.

As an Energy Being, I want you to take a quick scan of your body. See where you need energy and where you don't. The light areas are where you have it, the dark areas are where you need it. Send it out of your spirit like before, but this time I want you to send energy down to your body, and notice that as soon as you send it, it's being replenished by your Source, and your capacity to hold it has increased yet again! There is no limit to the number of people you can give this love to, including yourself, or how large a being you can become holding it.

Note: At this point they may realize that they have indeed separated from their body and are now fully ready to have an energy clearing. You then tell the client that he or she has a choice. They can either remain outside of their body or get back in—it's up to them.

Even if your client falls asleep during the visualization, continue with it. They are still "getting it" on some level. Their tendency to fall asleep also tells you the obvious—they need the rest! You are now ready to begin the healing session, starting at the person's feet and working your way up to the top of their head.

*"Don't think you can attain total awareness
and whole enlightenment
without proper discipline and practice.
This is egomania.
Appropriate rituals channel your emotions
and life energy toward the light.
Without the discipline to practice them,
you will tumble constantly backward
into darkness."—Lao-tzu*

Chapter 16

Putting It All Together:
Outline of a Healing Session from Start to Finish

- Clear yourself out before your clients arrive
- Greet them cheerfully when they get there
- Offer them something to drink (tea, water)
- Point out the bathroom facilities
- Lead them into your healing room
- Do a consultation
- Have them sign any consent forms (see sample on page 183)
- Ask them to turn off their cell phone
- Collect your fee (getting this out of the way now will prevent distraction from the wonderful state they will be experiencing upon leaving)
- Ask them to remove their shoes, belts, etc.
- Help them to get comfortable on the table
- Ask if they have an aversion to being touched
- Show them where you will be placing your hands
- Find some aspect of them to love unconditionally
- Start music
- Silently ask for protection
- Do "Layers" Guided Visualization

- Do "The Ultimate Relaxation" Visualization
- Do "Melting" Visualization
- Start out at their feet
- Breathe; Relax; Connect to your sources of energy and to your client's; Tune-in to your own guidance; Be willing to accept any outcome
- In addition to anything else you find:
- Address any fear in their second chakra
- Address any anger in their third chakra
- Address any pain and heartbreak in their fourth chakra
- Get them to forgive themselves & others
- Work your way to the top of their head allowing your intuition to guide you as to the length of each stop
- When finished, smooth out, puff up and rake through their auric field
- Allow them time to lie there and reflect on what has just occurred
- Offer them a refreshment
- Ask if there's anything which they'd like to share
- Escort them out
- Let them know that you will be following-up in a few days with a phone call to see how they're doing
- Clear yourself of negative energy
- Make a brief record of their visit, along with any issues that came up in session
- Make note on your calendar to place a follow-up phone call

Chapter 17

Finding Your Purpose in Life (Getting What You Want)

D ecades ago I worked for a large corporation in charge of a small group of creative people. I had a boss who was never satisfied with things the way they were. Whenever operations were organized and running smoothly, he would always reshuffle the department. At times he seemed to enjoy watching people scramble and panic to complete their ever-changing jobs. After a few years, and accomplishing every impossible task he threw at me, I began having chest pains that lasted for a couple of weeks. At times it felt like an elephant was sitting on my chest and those pains shot down my left arm and up the side of my neck.

One morning my boss came into my office with a file folder full of memos, stacked four inches high. He plopped them on my desk and said, "You have a meeting with your staff in an hour. I want you to read all those memos, plan out what each person will be doing over the next six months and tell them all at the meeting." In looking back, even if I had a week, this would have been a very complicated task. True to form, however, I simply took it on without question.

A minute or two later the chest pains started. I made a quick call to the health office to schedule a check-up at lunch time. When the nurse heard the symptoms she immediately gave the phone to the doctor in charge. He told me to get over there right away. I explained about my important meeting and hung up. He called back and pleaded with me to come over, saying that it would only take a couple of minutes. When I began to argue, he threatened to send over an ambulance. I finally gave in and went over. He did a quick EKG and said, "You're going to the hospital." My immediate response was "But my meeting!"

This is a perfect example of how we can lose track of our priorities. My body was clearly trying to tell me something, but I just wasn't listening. Fortunately there was nothing seriously wrong, but it took that experience to make me realize that had I dropped dead at that moment, my boss would have replaced me the next day. I had been lying to myself about how miserable I was at that job.

Many of us today are in very stressful situations. The only *real* security that we have is inside of us. Choosing to live a life that gives us joy is the first step to finding that security. If you're doing something you love, you will be more productive, healthier and happier. Doing what feels *right* positively affects the body, mind and spirit—and the people around us. Furthermore, by surrounding yourself with people who you love and who love you, can't help but make you feel even more fulfilled.

Make a List

Here's an assignment for those of you who are trying to find their purpose in life. Obviously, if you don't have a goal, it will be hard or even impossible to attain it. My belief is that we are each so spiritually unique, what may be right for one person might not be for another. So, how do you choose a direction that's perfect for you? Interests and passions! They are unique to each of us and are there for a reason.

Make a list of all the things that drive your passion for living. List things like food, sex, environments, types of people, anything and everything that makes you feel good! Each day take out the list, focus on it, read it over and add to it, maybe getting more specific as you progress. By just focusing on those things that make us happy, we are enlisting the Universe to bring them into our lives. In a sense we are co-creators of our own destiny.

I did this many years ago, listing things like being at home, working one-on-one with people, touching people and their lives, counseling people, plants, water, sacred spaces, stained glass, candles, crystals, relaxing music, and being near the refrigerator. Just about every item on my list is now, in some way, included in my healing room (with the exception of the refrigerator). These were listed long before I ever heard of hands-on energy healing! In an odd way, it seemed as if the Universe had created and tailored that occupation just for me. We are all a lot more powerful than we think. Our thoughts are constantly creating our reality. By steadily focusing on what we want, rather than what we don't, we can create any reality we desire.

Exactly Where You're Supposed to Be!

When is the last time you took the opportunity to relax and feel your connection to everything around you? Close your eyes now and feel your true connection to the Universe. Feel gratitude as you feel the love inside of you extending outward—feel the love from the Universe entering you in a never-ending cycle. You will realize that there are no accidents or coincidences and that everything is perfect in it's own imperfection.

I had heard stories a while ago about some of the survivors of the Twin Towers disaster and why they had survived. For one fellow it was his turn to buy donuts—and so he was late. One of my clients had a toothache that day and went to the dentist instead. Another fellow was delayed because his son started kindergarten. Still another decided to wear a new pair of shoes that morning and developed a blister on the way to work. He was late because he stopped at a drug store to buy a bandage.

Try to remember that the next time you get angry standing in a checkout line or frustrated behind a slow driver. There could be a very good reason for it—there always is! You are *exactly* where you're supposed to be at any given time. By realizing this fact you are consciously raising your awareness level—and fulfilling your own destiny.

Our destiny is like a long river taking us down a unique path loaded with twists and turns, each mapped out long before we came here. If you choose to fight against the current, you will find yourself exhausted, depressed and unhappy. By learning to accept your path, using the current to your own advantage, and listening to your inner guidance or intuition, you will gain a clearer vision of why you chose to come here in the first place. Sometimes your river converges with someone else's and you find yourself fortunate enough to make part or all of the remaining journey with them. Your free will allows you to decide when to stop, which side of the river to visit and which opportunities to take or overlook as you progress. Enjoy your life! You were meant to. As you feel more fulfilled, that feeling will rub off on those around you. It can't help but do so because everything is energy and we are all intimately connected.

You are the Healer!

Energy healing is an intimately shared experience, and unconditional love *is* the essence that heals! It's the substance that makes up all of the healing energy I've discussed. Learning to love *unconditionally* is the one spiritual goal that we all have in common. It might just be our main reason for being here on this planet right now— especially during these times. There's a saying among healers that you can't heal someone you don't love. Make it *your* goal to find some aspect to love in each person you meet.

It's not always easy, but you can achieve far more in every aspect of your life by showing unconditional kindness, consideration, compassion and gratitude to everyone who enters your life than by any other means. Be proud of your own radiant spirit and don't be afraid to share that beautiful part of you with everyone who enters your life. Remember, YOU ARE THE HEALER and the world is a better place because of you!

"People of the world don't look at themselves,
and so they blame one another."
—Rumi

SAMPLE CONSENT FORM

(Please check with your own attorney regarging the specific wording, terminology and legality of such a form in your area).

This form is an explanation as well as an agreement between the client and the healer. I believe that healing comes from within. My purpose is to assist in that healing through various practices, including energy healing techniques with my hands on the body as well as working on the energy field which surrounds the body. These will help to balance your energy, enhance your sense of well-being, and increase your self-awareness.

I am not a physician and therefore do not diagnose disease or prescribe drugs. I will not advise you to discontinue medical treatment you may be receiving. My work is intended to be in harmony with traditional medicine or psychotherapy. Feel free to discuss our work with your physician or therapist. I may recommend dietary or lifestyle changes which you may choose to implement. In the course of our work we may discuss many of the issues which influence your emotional and physical well-being. These discussions will be kept confidential.

A fee for services is required. The fee for the first session is $_____ and is payable at the time of the treatment.

In signing this document, you agree that I will work with you in the manner described above. Most of my clients experience increased well-being and improvement in their physical and emotional condition. However, no promise of outcome can be made.

The client hereby acknowledges that he/she has read the forgoing CONSENT FOR TREATMENT, and is satisfied that he/she fully understands the nature of the treatments and freely elects to have the same. The client releases _____ _____ from any and all claims of malpractice, non-disclosure, or lack of informed consent.

Client's signature_____Date_____

Print name_____Telephone:(____)_____

Address_____

City_____State_____Zip_____

E-mail:_____

Suggested Reading:

Adler, Andrea. *Creating an Abundant Practice: A Spiritual and Practical Guide for Holistic Practitioners and Healing Centers.* Santa Fe: Self-Publihed, 2001

Beinfield, Harriet L.Ac. and Korngold, Efrem L.Ac. *Between Heaven and Earth: A Guide to Chinese Medicine.* New York: Ballantine Wellspring, 1991

Benjamin, Lorna Smith. *Interpersonal Diagnosis and Treatment of Personality Disorders.* New York: The Guilford Press, 1996

Blanchard, Kenneth, Ph.D. and Johnson, Spencer, MD. *The One Minute Manager.* New York: William Morrow and Company, Inc., 1982

Brennan, Barbara Ann. *Hands of Light: A Guide to Healing Through the Human Energy Field.* New York: Bantam Books, 1988

Bruyere, Rosalyn L. *Wheels of Light.* New York: Simon & Schuster, 1994

Campbell, Chellie. *The Wealthy Spirit: Daily Affirmations for Financial Stress Reduction.* Naperville, Illinois: Sourcebooks, Inc., 2002

Dyer, Dr. Wayne W. *The Power of Intention: Learning to Co-create Your World Your Way.* Carlsbad, California: Hay House Inc., 2004.

Easwaran, Eknath. *Meditation.* Tomales, California: Nilgiri Press, 1991

Eden, Donna. *Energy Medicine.* New York: Tarcher/Penguin, 1998

Grabhorn, Jean. *Excuse Me, Your Life Is Waiting: The Astonishing Power of Feelings.* Charlottesville, Virginia: Hampton Roads Publishing Company, Inc., 2000

Gerber, Richard, MD. *Vibrational Medicine.* Rochester, Vermont: Bear & Company, 2001

Hanh, Thich Nhat. *The Long Road Turns To Joy: A Guide to Walking Meditation.* Berkeley, California: Parallax Press, 1996

Hay, Louise L. *Heal Your Body A–Z.* Carlsbad, California: Hay House Inc., 1998

Judith, Anodea. *Eastern Body Western Mind, Psychology and the Chakra System as a Path to the Self.* Berkeley, California: Celestial Arts, 1996

Kornfield, Jack. *After the Ecstacy, the Laundry.* New York: Bantam Books, 2000

Khader, Dina MS, RD, CDN. *The Food Combining/Blood Type Diet Solution.* Australia: Keats Publishing, 2000

Laskow, Leonard, MD. *Healing with Love, A Breakthrough Mind/Body Medical Program for Healing Yourself and Others.* Mill Valley, California: Wholeness Press, 1992

Linn, Denise. *Altars: Bringing Sacred Shrines Into Your Daily Life.* New York: Ballantine Wellspring, 1999

McWade, Miki. *Getting Up, Getting Over, Getting On: A Twelve Step Guide to Divorce Recovery.* Beverly Hills, California: Champion Press, Ltd., 2000

McWade, Miki. *Daily Meditations For Surviving a Breakup, Separation or Divorce.* Beverly Hills, California: Champion Press, Ltd., 2002

Myss, Caroline, Ph.D. *Energy Anatomy: The Science of Personal Power, Spirituality, and Health.* Sounds True, Inc., 1996.

Newton, Michael. *Journey of Souls.* St. Paul, Minnesota: Llewellyn Publications, 2000

Orloff, Judith, M.D. *Positive Energy: 10 Extraordinary Prescriptions For Transforming Fatigue, Stress & Fear Into Vibrance, Strength & Love.* New York: Harmony Books, 2004

Oz, Mehmet, M.D. *Healing form the Heart.* New York: Plume/Penguin, 1999

Yen, Ming-Sun, MD, Chiang, Joseph, MD, Chen, Myrna Louison. *Buddhist Healing Touch.* Rochester, Vermont: Healing Arts Press, 2001

Weiss, Brian MD. *Messages from the Masters: Tapping into the Power of Love.* New York: Warner Books, 2000

Welwood, John. *Love and Awakening.* New York: HarperPerennial, 1996

Wendy! *The Naked Quack: Exposing the Many Ways Phony Psychics and Mediums Cheat You.* New York: Chanworth Global Enterprises, 2000

Music Resources:

Aeoliah *Angel Love*

Coxon, Robert Haig *The Silent Path*

Fitzgerald, Scott *Solitude*

Halpern, Steven *Inner Peace*

John, Werner *The Healing Flute*

Merlin's Magic: The Heart of Reiki

Secret Garden *White Stones*

2002 *This Moment Now*

2002 *Land of Forever*

2002 *River of Stars*

The Motion Picture Soundtrack from *A Beautiful Mind*

Index

With gratitude, respect and admiration...

I would like to thank the following marvelous people for their role in my life, for supporting my healing practice and for encouraging me to write this book:

Maria Bennett, Ph.D., one of my closest friends and one of the most talented, intelligent and humblest writers I've ever had the honor and priviledge to work with. Without her generous help, endless patience, loving encouragement, dedication, guidance, moral support, kind and thoughtful inspiration early into this project, this book would not have come to fruition.

Donna Baker Church, one of the most truly talented editor/writers I've ever had the pleasure to work with. Her caring, sensitive, spiritually based editing style plus her loyal, generous and warm friendship continue to be a source of inspiration, information, professionalism, organization, amazement and gratitude. She made the editing process a joyful adventure!

Elaine Hjelte, MS, a very special friend and fellow healer over many years. Her continued encouragement, occasional teaching partnership and constant presence in my life are an on-going source of gratitude.

Katherine Vockins, a very dear and kind friend whose marketing genius, writing and organizational abilities continually encourage and inspire me to move ahead in many areas. She is a true example of the effects of unconditional love on all those who are lucky enough to be touched by her life.

Susan Barry, MHT, one of the best hypnotherapists, past-life, and in-between life regressionists there is. Her continued friendship, trust, belief, healing partnership and loyal support has always been there for me. Susan was the first to host my workshops in her own offices, and continues to do so.

Carol Milove, whose belief in my talents enabled me to do my first workshop many years ago as part of a continuing education program which she founded and whose ongoing friendship serves as a cherished blessing.

Micki McWade, MSW, for being the first to ask me to lecture on healing at the12 Step Divorce Recovery Programs which she founded plus inspiring me as a successful author and therapist. She is also a pioneer in Collaborative Divorce, has been a steadfast personal friend for countless years and has often honored me by referring her own clients to me.

Wendy!, One of my longest friends and one of the most gifted Psychics on the planet. Wendy is also one of the nicest, most caring and personable individuals you're likely to meet anywhere.

Ginny Vreeland, BSN, MA, for her long-term healing friendship, inspiration, loving support and encouragement. Ginny volunteered to read this book in its early stages. Her awesome spiritual gifts plus her tireless energy and ceaseless dedication to all those in need always has and continues to amaze me.

Roberta Apuzzo, a generous and kind friend, for her continued support over the years demonstrated by having me on her radio talk show many times.

Marge Lovero, one of the most inspiring and knowledgeable entrepreneurial teachers of our time. A friend who has also had me as a guest on her talk show.

Wendy L. Hurwitz, MD, a delightful, caring, gifted and valued friend. A top stress management consultant, teacher and medical intuitive who, among other things, has an astounding ability to sense and diagnose energy. Her down-to-earth, loving presence coupled with her extensive knowledge, wisdom and sense of humor are everything anyone could want in a good friend and business associate.

Andrea Adler, for her trusting friendship. Andrea is a public relations and publishing expert who gave of her time and knowledge freely. She is a shining example of what the power of intention and being in harmony with the Universe can do.

Rev. Janice Rost, a wonderfully experienced healer in many modalities, long-time friend and ally whose exercise I adapted to form "See the Spirit."

Kathanna Knapp, an extraordinary master energy healer and friend, whose "intuition" and "leg healing" exercises are listed in this book.

Leisha Douglas, Ph. D., a wonderful friend, marvelously sensitive intuitive, and therapist. Her thoughtful observations in many areas have always been enlightening. We also refer our clients to each other from time to time.

Andrea Candee, MH, MSC, for her warm friendship, generous help, encouragement and insightful suggestions over many years.

Barbara Chintz, a true publishing promotional professional, master editor, writer and valued friend. Her observations and suggestions were appreciated.

Michael Rosenbaum, ACHP, a generous, warm, caring master healer, hypnotherapist & friend whom I learned a lot from by just being in his presence. One of his guided visualizations was a basis and inspiration for my own.

Rev. Helen Celestine Escofier, a wonderful spiritual teacher and practitioner whose life focus has always been on helping others.

Michael Finkelstein, MD, FACP, ABHM, who believed in me enough to ask me to work on-staff with him. He is truly one of the kindest, most decent and caring people on the planet. I am proud to call him a friend.

Sara Rubin, a marvelous master healer, and mystic whom I honor as my first Hands-on teacher. A few of the exercises in this book were adapted from Sara's original exercises for which I am grateful.

Lisa Grey, for being one of the first to read my initial manuscript and to offer very constructive criticism. Her uplifting friendship, caring sensitivity and brilliance are qualities that I continue to treasure.

Ed McClelland, a master healer in many areas, whose continuing cheerful encouragement, scientific validation and sense of humor is appreciated.

Roberta Russell, a good friend, sensitive and masterful healer in many modalities who has always offers sincere, kind, supportive words. She exhudes beautiful energy in everything she does.

Janine Fleury, a wonderful Reiki Master, hypnotherapist and friend whose warm and charismatic presence is a delight to all who know her.

Virginia Roebuck, a master massage therapist and healer whose beautiful, calm, warm, vibrant energy has to be experienced to be believed. Her truly unique friendship is a wonderful blessing.

Cindy Blum, MS, CHT, PLRT, and **Mark Banschek MD**, both master healers in their own modalities, for their generous inspiration, friendship and continued successful efforts at bringing various facets of the healing community together. They are two of the most generous people on the planet.

Rev. Rosalyn Bruyere, Judith Orloff, MD, Caroline Myss, Ph.D., and so many others who gave me some of the tools with which to do my work.

Thanks also to my many other friends, clients, and students who although they haven't been mentioned here, I am truly grateful for their presence in my life. They have been and continue to be my best teachers.

For more information regarding
Gene Krackehl's upcoming workshops
or to schedule a personal healing session,
please visit:

www.AmazingHealer.com

or e-mail Gene:
Gene@AmazingHealer.com

Order Form

To order more copies of **YOU ARE THE HEALER**
please fill out and mail the form below or visit our website:
www.InnerPlacePublishing.com

No. of Copies_____ x $19.95   = $ _____

                  Subtotal: = $ _____

Sales Tax: *Add 7.5% of subtotal for books shipped to New York addresses only*   = $ _____

Shipping & $4.00 first book   = $ _____
Handling

                $1.00 each add'l book   = $ _____

              Total: = $ _____

Name: _____

Address: _____

City: _____

State: _____ Zip _____ E-mail: _____

Payment Enclosed: ❏ Personal Check   ❏ Money Order

Mail to: Inner Place Publishing   E-mail questions or
             P.O. Box 374   comments to:
             Katonah, NY 10536   Info@InnerPlacePublishing.com

All funds must be made in U.S. Dollars. For credit card orders and shipping outside the United States please see our website.